DEFENCE ACQUISITION PROCESS

A Systems View

DEFENCE ACQUISITION PROCESS

A Systems View

Brigadier Vikram Taneja

KNOWLEDGE WORLD
KW Publishers Pvt Ltd
New Delhi

Centre for Land Warfare Studies
Delhi Cantt
New Delhi

The Centre for Land Warfare Studies (CLAWS), New Delhi, is an autonomous think tank dealing with contemporary issues of national security and conceptual aspects of land warfare, including conventional and sub-conventional conflicts and terrorism. CLAWS conducts research that is futuristic in outlook and policy-oriented in approach.

Centre for Land Warfare Studies
RPSO Complex, Parade Road, Delhi Cantt, New Delhi 110010
Tel: +91.11.25691308 **Fax:** +91.11.25692347
Email: landwarfare@gmail.com **Website:** www.claws.in
CLAWS Army No. 33098

Disclaimer: The contents of this book are based on the analysis of materials accessed from open sources and are the personal views of the author. The contents, therefore, may not be quoted or cited as representing the views or policy of the Government of India, or Integrated Headquarters of MoD (Army), or the Centre for Land Warfare Studies.

ISBN 978-93-86288-45-5 Hardback
ISBN 978-93-86288-46-2 ebook

Published in India by Kalpana Shukla

KW Publishers Pvt Ltd
4676/21, First Floor, Ansari Road
Daryaganj, New Delhi 110002
Phone: +91 11 23263498/43528107
Marketing: kw@kwpub.com
Editorial: jose@kwpub.com
Website: www.kwpub.com

2011 FPBA BEST PUBLISHERS AWARD (ENGLISH)

Printed and bound by Rajkamal Electric Press.

CONTENTS

List of Abbreviations vii

Acknowledgements xiii

Preface xv

1. Modernisation Shapes and Contours 1

2. Overview of Defence Capital Acquisition System 27

3. Systemic Problems in the Acquisition System 61

4. A Systems Approach to Defence Capital Acquisitions in India 117

5. Programme Management Structure for Defence Acquisitions: The Way Forward 139

LIST OF ABBREVIATIONS

AAD	Army Air Defence
AAP	Annual Acquisition Plan
ADG	Additional Director General
ADG PI	Additional Director General Public Information
AoN	Acceptance of Necessicity
AST	Anti-Satellite
ATAGS	Advanced Towed Artillery Gun System
AMLS	Acquisition Manager Land Systems
ARMD	Armoured Corps
ARTY	Artillery
BCG	Boston Consulting Group
BOA	Basic Ordering Agreement
BE	Budget Estimates
BHEL	Bharat Electronics Limited
BMS	Battlefield Management System
CAG	Comptroller and Auditor General
CAS	Chief of the Air Staff
CCS	Cabinet Committee on Security
CDG	Capability Development Group
CDM	Capability Development Managers
CDP	Capability Development Plan
CDS	Chief of the Defence Staff
CDE	Capability Development Executive
CEO	Chief Executive Officer
CFA	Competent Financial Authority
CLAWS	Centre for Land Warfare Studies
CINCCDE	Commander-in-Chief Capability Development Executive
CoSP	Chief of Strategic Priorities

CNC	Commercial Negotiation Committee
CPFR	Collaborative Planning Forecasting Replenishment
CRP	Continuous Replenishment Programme
COAS	Chief of the Army Staff
COSC	Chief of Staff Committee
COTS	Commercially Off the Shelf
CNS	Chief of the Naval Staff
CVC	Chief Vigilance Commissioner
DA	Defence Attache
DAC	Defence Acquisition Council
DAD	Defence Accounts Department
DARPA	Defence Advanced Research Projects Agency
DAU	Defence Acquisition University
DAW	Defence Acquisition Wing
DAWIA	Defence Acquisition Workforce Improvement Act
DCOAS (P&S)	Deputy Chief of the Army Staff (Planning and Systems)
DCP	Defence Capability Plan
DCIDS	Deputy Chief of Integrated Defence Staff
DDP	Department of Defence Production
DG	Director General
DDG	Deputy Director General
DE&S	Defence Equipment and Support
DGA	Director General of Armamant (France)
DGQA	Director General of Quality Assurance
DIPP	Department of Industrial Policy and Promotion
DLO	Defence Logistics Organisation
DMO	Defence Material Organisation
DMCP	Defence Ministers Council on Production
DOD	Department of Defence
DPA	Defence Procurement Agency
DPP	Defence Procurement Procedure
DPS	Defence Planning Staff
DPSU	Defence Public Sector Undertaking
DPB	Defence Procurement Board

DTC	Defence Technology Council
EDI	Electronic Data Interface
EEZ	Exclusive Economic Zone
EMI	Electro-Magnetic Interference
EMC	Electro-Magnetic Compatibility
EME	Electronics and Mechanical Engineers
ENGRS	Engineers
EW	Electronic Warfare
FDI	Foreign Direct Investment
FIPB	Foreign Investment Promotion Board
FICV	Futuristic Infantry Combat Vehicle
FMS	Foreign Military Sales
FOS	Family of Systems
FTP	Fast Track Procedure
GCCCS	Global Combat Command Control System
GDP	Gross Domestic Product
GS EVAL	General Staff Evaluation
GSEPC	General Staff Equipment Policy Committee
GOM	Group of Ministers
HAL	Hindustan Aeronautics Limited
HVDP	High Value Defence Procurement
HQ	Headquarters
IAF	Indian Air Force
IAAS	Indian Audit and Accounts Service
ICBM	Inter-Continental Ballistic Missile
IDAS	Indian Defence Accounts Service
IDS	Integrated Defence Staff
IGA	Inter-Governmental Agreement
IPMT	Integrated Project Management Team
IRBM	Intermediate Range Ballistic Missile
INDU	Indian National Defence University
INF	Infantry
JSEPC	Joint Staff Equipment Policy Committee
JV	Joint Venture
KRC	Kargil Review Committee

LCC	Life Cycle Cost
LCH	Light Combat Helicopter
LD	Liquidated Damage
LTIPP	Long-Term Integrated Perspective Plan
LUH	Light Utility Helicopter
MA	Military Attache
MAA	Material Acquisition Agreement
MEA	Ministry of External Affairs
MET	Maintainability and Evaluation Trials
MECH	Mechanised Infantry
MHA	Ministry of Home Affairs
MoC	Ministry of Commerce
MoD	Ministry of Defence
MTOT	Maintenance Transfer of Technology
MMRCA	Medium Multi-Role Combat Aircraft
MI	Military Intelligence
NBC	Nuclear, Biological and Chemical Warfare
NSA	National Security Adviser
NDC	National Defence College
NEFA	North-East Frontier Agency
OEM	Original Equipment Manufacturer
OFB	Ordnance Factory Board
OF	Ordnance Factory
PBL	Performance-Based Logistics
PEO	Project Executive Officer
PD 2	Procurement Desktop 2
PIF	Project Initiation Forum
PLA	People's Liberation Army
PMO	Project Management Organisation
PP DTE	Perspective Planning Directorate
PP&FD	Perspective Planning and Force Development
PPP	Public Private Participation
QCBS	Quality-Cum-Cost-Based Systems
RACI	Responsibility, Accountability, Consultancy and Information

R&D	Research and Development
RE	Revised Allocation
RFI	Request For Information
RFP	Request For Proposal
RLD	Reverse Liquidated Damage
RM	Raksha Mantri
RRM	Rajya Raksha Mantri
SA TO RM	Scientific Adviser To Raksha Mantri
SAE	Service Acquisition Executive
SCAP	Services Capital Acquisition Plan
SCAP CC	Services Capital Acquisition Plan Categorisation Committee
SCAPCHC	Services Capital Acquisition Plan Categorisation Higher Committee
SDPG	Strategic Defence Planning Guidance
SDR	Stragetic Defence Review
SHQ	Service Headquarters
SIPRI	Stockholm International Peace Research Institute
SME	Small and Medium Enterprise
SRM	Suppliers Relations Management
SSM	Soft Systems Methodology
SLBM	Submarine Launched Ballistic Missile
SQR/	Services Qualitative Requirement/General
GSQR/QR	Services Qualitative Requirement/Qualitative Requirement
SQR DG	SQR Development Group
TCA	Total Cost of Acquisition
TCS	Tactical Communications System
TEC	Technical Evaluation Committee
TRM	Task Responsibility Matrix
TPCR	Technology Perspective Capability Roadmap
TPR	Technical Project Report
TOEC	Technical Offset Evaluation Committee
UAV	Unmanned Aerial Vehicle

USD (AT&L)	Under-Secrtary of Defence (Acquisition Technology & Logistics)
UNPKO	UN Peace-Keeping Operations
VCOAS	Vice Chief of the Army Staff
VMI	Vendor Managed Inventory
WE DTE	Weapons and Equipment Directorate

ACKNOWLEDGEMENTS

It is a matter of great honour and privilege to have been bestowed the research opportunity on this topic of national importance which I am sanguine shall be of use to the practitioners and exponents of capital acquisition in the related spheres. It gives me immense personal satisfaction and pride to have interacted with my esteemed colleagues and seniors whose benevolent assistance, suggestions, inspiration and cooperation encouraged me to complete this research.

I would like to express my deep sense of gratitude to Lt Gen BS Nagal, PVSM, AVSM, SM (Retd), Director, Centre for Land Warfare Studies (CLAWS), for his consistent guidance, sublime suggestions and constructive approach during the course of my investigation without which this research would not have been possible.

I would also like to convey my sincere gratitude to Brig KS Sheoran, Additional Director at CLAWS, for his keen interest and intellectual guidance throughout the period of this study. I would also like to thank Brig Vinod Dutta, DACIDS, HQ Integrated Defence Staff (IDS), Brig Sanjay Sethi, Commandant Central Ammunition Depot, Pulgaon, Col Vikas Rohilla, Director Master General of the Ordnance Branch, Col Badal Sheopuri, Director Perspective Planning (AoN and Categorisation), and Col Anuraag Chhibber, formerly at the Weapons and Equipment Directorate and presently Senior Fellow and Scholar at CLAWS for their practical suggestions on the complex subject of capital acquisitions. I would like to convey my sincere thanks to Gp Capt CR Mohan VSM, Indian Air Force, who had laid the foundations of this research, and without whose contribution, this research would not have become a reality.

I am also thankful to the Commandant and faculty of the College of Defence Management, Secunderabad, for their support and inspiration and, finally, to Col Amar Singh, Director, Military Training, for facilitating the research.

Delhi Cantt **Vikram Taneja**
April 2016

PREFACE

The performance of the existing defence capital acquisition system in the past few decades has been sub-optimal, leading to hollowness in terms of weapons and equipment holdings with the Army. Procedural refinements, in terms of regular Defence Procurement Procedure (DPP) revisions have not enhanced the effectiveness of the acquisition system. A deeper study reveals a failure of the acquisition system to perform optimally due to the absence of the requisite structures and models under the Ministry of Defence (MoD) to execute the DPP effectively. The symptoms of the problems are manifested in the inability of the armed forces to modernise as per the Long-Term Integrated Perspective Plan (LTIPP), huge time delays in procurement, denying the forces their legitimate equipment authorisation, cost over-runs, resulting in lower availability in successive years, delayed booking of funds, often leading to their surrender, the thick web of bureaucratic procedures, and lack of accountability,[1] and, finally, an inability to implement the recommendations of successive committees on acquisition reform.

Probable causes to which these symptoms can be attributed are: ineffective organisation, nominal coordination, no effective feedback mechanism to monitor modernisation of the forces at the functional level, lack of sensitivity about the urgency and criticality of equipment at all levels, lack of awareness and exposure of stakeholders in commercial and legal aspects, lack of effective decision-making and, lastly, over-dependence on Defence Public Sector Undertakings (DPSUs), as compared to the private sector.

The ensuing chapters examine India's defence capital acquisition procedure using the 'systems approach'. Any system is an identifiable, complex and dynamic entity, having an objective.

It is composed of discernible elements or sub-systems. These are related to, and inter-dependent on, each other; and the whole element has an overall capability to maintain stability and to adapt behaviour in response to external influences. A system exists because it is designed to achieve one or more objectives[2]. The objective of the system designed for facilitating smooth capital acquisition could be to ensure timely procurement of military equipment, systems, and platforms as required by the armed forces in terms of performance capabilities and quality standards, through optimum utilisation of allocated budgetary resources; and, while enabling the same, the highest degree of probity, public accountability, transparency, fair competition and a level playing field will be provided for. In addition, the aim of self-reliance in defence equipment production and acquisition will be steadfastly pursued. This, in fact, is the stated aim of the recently released DPP 2016. The research put forth in this book is focused more towards analysis of the acquisition system using systems approach in the process examine its deficits. Collegiate efforts of all stakeholders primarily the Service Head Quarters and MoD, have given way to DPP 2016 which on its part recommends certain far reaching changes that need time to stabilize and are expected to enhance the performance of the capital acquisition systems.

Present performance of the acquisition system, has its roots in a number of objective and subjective issues. A preliminary examination of the problem through the "Jackson and Keys", systems situation grid,[3] discussed at length in the present research, indicates that relevant systems in the context of the situation could be classified as a complex–pluralist problem situation. The complexity of the system denotes a large number of sub-systems involved in fulfilling the user's aspirations. On the other hand, the pluralistic nature indicates that all the participants of the system share compatible interests *but may not share common values and beliefs and, consequently, lack consensus on the methodology to be adopted to achieve the ends, which is very apt for the acquisition system,* more than ever before. The structures, processes and cultural issues applied by various parties themselves often lack congruence, causing counter-productive and sub-optimal outcomes. It is, thus, established that the soft systems approach will be more suitable for resolving the subject problem situation than linear thinking wherein the problem is broken down into smaller sub-parts to arrive at solutions in a sequential manner and, then, finally, reassembled/reintegrated. The present system of acquisition has been examined by using the Soft System Methodology (SSM). Initially, an analysis of the rich picture has been carried out and thereafter, task and issue-based analysis has been done. The task-based analysis focusses on ways to enhance the availability of weapons and equipment while preventing time and cost over-runs. The relevant systems and root definitions were culled out from the above issues identified from the rich picture and are discussed in detail in the subsequent chapters. This 'Relevant System' pertains to the structural interface between various stakeholders involved in the acquisition process. The specific questions that any researcher delving into the field of acquisition research must answer are: *firstly,* will more major changes in procurement procedures result in enhanced and timely procurements? *Secondly*, will a change in the organisational structure and change in the interaction between various stakeholders of the acquisition system for procurement result in more effective and timely procurements? *Thirdly*, will building structures into the acquisition system to bring in greater responsibility and accountability improve the time taken to process procurement cases? *Fourthly*, will the resolution of interests of various stakeholders result in speedy acquisitions? And, *lastly*, what other changes in the organisational structure and processes are required to ensure timely modernisation of the Armed forces?

Answers to the above questions have been sought by means of a primary research by fielding a survey instrument based on the postulates on the systems approach given by George Wilhelm Hegel (1770-1831), a German philosopher who is credited as being a pioneer in systems thinking. The overall survey looked at three constructs, i.e. the process, the structure and the readiness among the acquisition stakeholders to accept change. The populations and establishments from whom data was desired were, firstly, the relevant officers in the Service Headquarters (SHQ) and Headquarters Integrated Defence Staff (HQ IDS) dealing with acquisition; secondly, the MoD to include the Director General (DG) Acquisition, and thereafter, the officials from the DPSUs and private sector dealing in acquisitions. Lastly, data was also sought from the officers undergoing the National Defence College (NDC) course so as to get an independent view from the users.

Structure of the Book

The book is laid out over a total of five chapters. Chapter 1 examines the need for modernisation as a result of India's geo-political realities. Chapter 2 discusses the existing acquisition system in detail, along with the historical background, the evolution of the DPP, the existing procurement organisation and the overall performance of the acquisition system. Chapter 3 examines the output of the various sub-systems comprising the acquisition system, namely, the planning sub-system, the budgetary sub-system and the supply chain management aspects. Chapter 4 approaches the acquisition system from the paradigm of a systems approach and Chapter 5 examines the existing acquisition structures and suggests a programme management structure in detail and, finally, suggests the way ahead.

Notes

1. Robin David, "The Ministry of Defence is a Bad Organisation with No Accountability: Gen V P Malik," TNN, December 20, 2016, http://timesofindia.indiatimes.com/india/The-ministry-of-defence-is-a-bad-organisation-with-no-accountability-Gen-V-P-Malik/articleshow/50251687.cms
2. Peter M Senge, *The Fifth Discipline, The Art and Science of The Learning Organisation* (Random House Business Books, 2006).
3. Robert L Flood, *Dealing with Complexity: An Introduction to the Theory and Application of Systems Science* (Springer Science and Business Media, March 31, 1993).

1. MODERNISATION SHAPES AND CONTOURS

> The threats may be known, but the enemy may be invisible. *Domination of cyber space will become increasingly important. Control of space may become as critical as that of land, air and sea. Full scale wars may become rare, but force will remain an instrument of deterrence and influencing behaviour, and the duration of conflicts will be shorter.*
>
> — Shri Narendra Modi, Prime Minister of India,
> Address to the Combined Commanders Conference,
> October 2014

The Indian acquisition ecosystem is reveling in its new-found vibrancy thanks to a beneficent infusion of fresh policy. The present government, since 2014, has cleared a substantial number of capital acquisition cases[1], and launched many enabling initiatives, resultantly ushering in a positive acquisition organisational climate. Though these measures will take time to transform into physical acquisitions[2] and, finally, into measurable capability, the ball has been set rolling and if the latest capital allocation to the Budget Estimates (BE) 2016-17 is disregarded[3], it can be assumed, albeit with some caution, that arming the Services remains a priority for the government.

On the other hand, unfolding of some major contracts beyond the 'in principal approval' of the Defence Acquisition Council (DAC) does not inspire much confidence in the end user. Priority one procurements such as that of assault rifles have been reset with the withdrawal of the Request for Proposal (RFP) in 2015.[4] The contract for bullet-proof jackets[5] urgently required by the Army still remains to be inked. Certain major acquisitions, namely, the M777 howitzer deal and the recently cleared utility helicopters for the Army are being progressed with Russia under the 'Make in India' programme,[6] bypassing the Defence Procurement Procedure (DPP) through the Inter-Governmental Agreement (IGA) or Foreign Military Sales (FMS) route which certainly does not augur well for the DPP's performance as India's all encompassing capability building document.

Extensive process reengineering is on the anvil with the new DPP 2016 already been promulgated in June 2016 [7]. The shape of things to come has cast a shadow through policy pronouncements such as the new offsets policy[8] that articulates enhancing the offsets threshold from the existing to INR 2,000 crore and the announcement of the introduction of IDDM (Indigenously Designed, Developed and Manufactured) equipment as a proposed category for acquisition. In essence, the revised DPP envisages to provide a boost to the government's 'Make in India' initiative, enhance the involvement of the private sector, build indigenous design and development capabilities, promote absorption of world-class technologies, provide premium consideration to high quality products, promote the growth of the Micro Small and Medium Enterprises (MSME) sector, and reduce timelines across various stages of procurement in addition to procedural refinements effected to enhance the efficiency and effectiveness of the procurement process[9].

The strategic scenario in the subcontinent was never more in India's favour, with Pakistan embroiled in a bitter campaign against a potent albeit nebulous adversary on its western frontiers. The country is also beset with a raging ethnic insurgency in Baluchistan. Karachi, the financial capital of the state, is seething with ethnic, sectarian and terrorist violence. Violence levels in southern Punjab are increasing and even Rawalpindi and Islamabad face the threat of suicide attacks. In 2014-15 itself, more than 4000 persons have been killed in terrorist violence perpetrated by the Tehrik-i-Taliban Pakistan (TTP) and its affiliates which denotes a phenomenal degree of violence. If analysts are to be believed, this campaign will be a long drawn one and is destined to keep the Pakistan

Army operationally deployed for a considerable period of time. Given this scenario, Pakistan, at least in the foreseeable future, does not have the capacity to pose a potent military threat to India. India, thus, has a window of opportunity available to kick-start its defence industrial infrastructure and produce fully indigenised tanks, artillery pieces and small arms for deployment on our western borders. While strategic considerations dictate importing urgently needed weaponry for deployment on our eastern borders, pouring billions of dollars into imports to fight an enemy which is neither willing nor able to challenge India in the near future is not reflective of sound statesmanship. Reforms at such a scale are only possible if India displays extraordinary leadership with an appetite for risk at both military and political levels, like the one which won us independence more than six decades ago. The recently released report of the "Committee[10] of Experts for amendment to DPP-2013, Including Formulation of a Policy Framework" by a ten-member eminent panel under Shri Dhirendra Singh, former Home Secretary, has recommended a policy framework for 'Make in India' in the defence sector which also forms a part of DPP 2016, released recently by the government.

Prime Minister Modi's recent address to the Combined Commanders aboard INS *Vikramaditya* in December 2015[11], aptly sums up India's strategic paradigm where he acknowledges India's tumultuous neighbourhood, with the full spectrum of security challenges. To quote, "India is subjected to terrorism and ceasefire violations; reckless nuclear build-up and threats; border transgressions; and continuing military modernisation and expansion. The shadow of West Asian instability is becoming longer. Beyond that, our region is marked by uncertain political transitions, weak institutions and internal conflicts, and major powers have also increased their engagement in our land and maritime neighbourhood". India, today, is seen not just as a new bright spot on the global economy but also as an anchor for regional and global peace, security and stability. As the world seeks to deal with the rising threat of terrorism and radicalism, countries across all regions, including in the Islamic world, have reached out to seek cooperation with India. India is also pursuing closer relations with China to harness the full potential of our economic partnership. India and China have the potential to engage constructively across the complexity of their relationship as two self-assured and confident nations, aware of their interests and responsibilities. India should continue to strengthen its defence capabilities and infrastructure, engage its neighbours more closely, and strengthen its regional and global partnerships, including in maritime security. The armed forces need to be ready for the future and have their perspective plans in sync with the financial realities.[12] India needs capabilities to win swift wars, as the days of the luxury of long drawn battles are over. There is a need to reform the structures of our armed forces and promote jointness at all levels.

Recent attempts to thaw relations between the two countries has been stymied by the Pakistan Army[13] with rhetoric[14] subverting the National Security Adviser (NSA) level talks planned in August 2015 between the two countries. The 2016 terror attacks on the Pathankot air base and later in Uri in J&K is an indicator of the sinister design of its non-state actors with the support of the Pakistani military establishment. Furthermore, China's collaboration with Pakistan continues to make things difficult for India. Pakistan openly uses terrorists to conduct a proxy war against India under its nuclear umbrella which is a cause of concern and has China's support, recently articulated, in blocking of India's move in the UN to include the Pathankot attack mastermind Masood Azhar in the UN sanctions list[15]. Pakistan's nuclear arsenal, developed with Chinese assistance, is by all accounts larger than India's and unlike India, it does not have a "no first use" policy. The recent bonhomie between Pakistan and Russia has also raised India's heckles.[16] China is going through a major military modernisation to make the People's Liberation Army (PLA) more lean and agile. To quote a report, "Never since 1949, have reforms been so drastic; one can mention the retrenchments of three lakh defence personnel, the reshuffle of the theatre commands, the setting up of a People's Liberation Army (PLA) Rocket Force and a Strategic Support Force or the 15 new departments, offices and commissions[17]". The PLA budget in the current fiscal year, surprisingly, has seen the lowest ever increase of 7.6 percent since 2010. However, the same still stands at a proposed US$ 146 billion[18] against an Indian budget of US$ 51 billion. Though it is deriving strength from the recent initiatives in a the US-Japan alliance to counter China in the South China Sea, India's support so far remains ideological and it has resisted recent US overtures for joint patrolling of the South China Sea along with the US, Japan and Australia[19]. Though India is building new relationships, it is still reluctant to form, or join, more robust institutional security frameworks. Instead of clear strategic thinking, India shuffles along, impeded by its caution and bureaucratic inertia. The symbol of these failings is India's reluctance to reform a defence-industrial base that wastes huge amounts of money, supplies the armed forces with sub-standard equipment and leaves the country dependent on imports for military modernisation[20]. India is presently the biggest importer of arms in the world, importing between 60 to 70 percent of its requirements[21]. The 'Make in India' initiative will take decades to fructify in terms of a regular free flow of equipment for the Services for which a recommended policy framework has just been promulgated. But as China forges ahead[22], India's strategic shortcomings are becoming a liability. And they are an obstacle to India's dreams of becoming a true 21st century global power[23]. India today is faced with an extensive defence and security perimeter, including 7,000 km of borders with countries with which major territorial disputes persist, a coastline of 7,600 km and 2.5 million sq km of Exclusive Economic Zone (EEZ) coupled with over 500 islands, and offshore hydrocarbon installations to protect. Security, today, has become all pervasive and holistic.

A country of India's size and international stature with

its present level of economic growth, perhaps cannot afford to ignore its security needs, therefore, vigilance and defence preparedness are imperative. India has the resources to do so. While the three arms of the defence forces are prepared for the defence of the country, several significant steps have been taken in the field of missile technology. Strategic commentators are of the view that this will add muscle to India's deterrence capacity against China. Although India has made commendable strides in nuclear capability, according to sources, "China's missile and nuclear arsenal is leagues ahead of India, capable as it is of hitting any city in India." India's entire focus is on building only credible minimum deterrence against China, not active offensive capabilities.

India's nuclear deterrence doctrine, it may be mentioned, revolves around a clear "no first use" policy[24]. A robust and survivable second-strike capability is hugely dependent on having nuclear-powered submarines, armed with Submarine-Launched Ballistic Missiles (SLBMs), which can operate silently under water for several months at a time. With the operationalisation of its nuclear submarine, India's is poised to achieve what is termed the nuclear triad[25], which means the capability to fire nuclear-tipped missiles from land, air and sea. As already stated, India's defence preparedness is purely defensive. India and China have very good political and diplomatic relations, and there are institutional and structural arrangements to deal with any untoward incident on the border and avoid any conflict. The resumption of defence exchanges between the two countries in June this year is symbolic of the keenness of the two countries to avoid any kind of tension. Trust and confidence between the military establishments of the two countries are essential for better relations; because, after all, security is not just a question of defence preparedness, but also a matter of mutual trust and confidence.

Controversy surrounding the leaked letter[26] written by the then Chief of the Army Staff (COAS) to the Prime Minister in 2011 describing the hollowness in defence preparedness had once again raised a vital question on the readiness of the defence forces to meet the ultimate eventualities for which billions of dollars of taxpayers' money are spent year after year. The concern is imperative for safeguarding the country's national security at a time when India's neighbours, particularly China, are undertaking massive military modernisation. After almost half a decade from the issue of that letter, very few capabilities have actually been deployed on the ground.

Defence planning in India has been rather disjointed and continues to be the same even in these times[27]. Despite efforts, there are glaring gaps between the three vital inter-related components of defence preparedness, namely plan, budget and procurement. A crucial recommendation of the Group of Ministers (GoM) for setting up a Chief of Defence Staff (CDS) entrusted with the task of, *inter alia*, preparing an integrated plan for the three Services and ensuring the holistic development of national military capability through inter and intra-Service prioritisation, is yet to be fully implemented. Instead, an ad hoc arrangement in the form of HQ Integrated Defence Staff (HQ IDS) has been instituted, perceived as ineffective in bringing the desired rigour into defence planning. In the absence of a CDS, the attempt so far seems to be driven by what may be called budget maximisation through big-ticket purchases by individual Services rather than focusing on the critical gaps that exist in the defence forces. On top of this, the present planning mechanism lacks an effective monitoring system to ensure that whatever plan has been prepared by the individual Services has actually been implemented. Reports now indicate that a four-star CDS based on recommendations of the 2012 Naresh Chandra Committee Report may be sanctioned soon[28]. The efficacy of this system will be seen in the times to come.

The critical shortages in the Army's combat power are long known[29]. The efforts should, therefore, have been made long before the current situation reached an alarming proportion. The deficiency in planning is further aggravated by the absence of long-term resource commitment by the government. Unlike some other countries which guarantee a steady flow of resources to defence over a period of five years or more, India's commitment does not go beyond a year. Moreover, the annual commitment is contingent upon a variety of factors, including the economic and fiscal situations of the prevalent year. The weakness of planning and budgeting has been further been aggravated by the deficiencies in the procurement system that the Ministry of Defence (MoD) has been desperately trying to overcome since the early Nineties. The MoD has expended a great deal of effort in putting up a defence procurement organisation and revising its procurement procedures for both revenue and capital items. These efforts have, no doubt, succeeded to a large extent, but much more needs to be done to enhance the ministry's ability to spend a majority of its allocated resources.

There are certain weaknesses in the system that have prohibited it from spending its full allotted budget. A trend analysis of the modernisation budget would indicate that the Services have surrendered a cumulative amount of nearly INR 28,000 crore between 2001-02 and 2010-11[30]. The Army's share alone was INR 6,000 crore in 2015-16[31]. It is this unspent money that has created an inexplicable hollowness in the planned modernisation of the armed forces. There are several weak areas in the procurement system that explain the surrender of funds and hollowness in defence preparedness. The first and foremost pertains to the ways the Qualitative Requirements (QRs) of equipment are being formulated. It is noteworthy that QRs are not only the starting point of the procurement process but the most vital part in terms of determining the most cost-efficient equipment in a time-bound manner. Deficiency in QR formulation could lead to either retraction of bids, hence, causing a delay, or costly procurement through uncompetitive bids. The importance of this component has so far drawn little attention from the policy-makers, despite repeated concerns raised by various oversight agencies. In 2007, the Comptroller and Auditor General (C&AG) of India in a performance audit report, Number 4 of 2007, on the Army's capital acquisition,[32] had observed that in many procurement contracts, the QRs were found to be "unrealistic with respect to actual requirements", "inconsistent with the technology available" and at times "unimportant, unverifiable and non-measureable". Seven years after the C&AG observations, the situation today does not seem to have changed for the better. In recent reports submitted to Parliament in December 2014 and April 2015, the standing committee nearly repeats the story narrated by C&AG in its report. The report, among other issues, also pertains to the Army's procurement of artillery guns, a critical void as far as its present firepower is concerned.

The standing committee's report highlights the Army's failure for four years in deciding on the features of the artillery it wants. It is noteworthy that the failure to freeze the requirements is not due to the rigidities of the procurement procedures, but due to the indecisiveness of the Army itself. Another major weakness in the procurement system is accountability. Although there has been an attempt at ensuring accountability by way of prescribing a detailed timeframe for each of the procurement functions, it has, however, not been successful. In the present procurement process, the acquisition functions are diffused between the Service Headquarters (SHQ) and the acquisition wing of the MoD. The Director General (Acquisition), who heads the acquisition wing and is considered the head of capital procurement, does not have the full responsibility to ensure accountability, as many of the acquisition functions, such as formulation of QRs, trials, etc, are beyond its power and purview. In other words, if something goes wrong, there is not a single authority other than the Defence Minister, who can be held accountable. The biggest accountability issue, however, comes when a procurement case comes under the scanner of oversight agencies such as the Central Vigilance Commission (CVC) and Central Bureau of Investigation (CBI). In such cases, decisions are kept in abeyance till the end of investigations, which in India takes longer than desired. To make matters worse, the MoD till recently was following an ill-conceived method of blacklisting firms found guilty of corrupt practices from doing business for a certain number of years rather than penalising them monetarily for their wrongdoing. As of 2015-16, the ministry has 15 companies, including six manufacturers, blacklisted and as many as 23 companies are under the scanner on allegations of corruption[33].Things are, however, looking up with the latest change in this policy in the offing.

The broad array of challenges to the national security in the fast changing geo-strategic security environment mandate a periodical reappraisal of the security procedures to cope with them. The government, keeping this in view, instituted a comprehensive review of the National Security System in its entirety for the first time in the history of independent India. The review was carried out by a Group of Ministers (GoM) constituted on April 17, 2000. The GoM consisted of the Home Minister, the Raksha Mantri, the External Affairs Minister and the Finance Minister. The GoM made recommendations regarding reforms in defence management. The process of implementation of the recommendations was initiated in 2001. These reforms have brought about improvements in the organisations, structures and processes for the integration of civil and military components.

The government also set up a Defence Acquisition Council (DAC) headed by the Raksha Mantri (RM) for decision-making in regard to the totality of the new planning process, which *inter-alia* involves according 'in principle' approval of capital acquisitions in the Long-Term Perspective Plan (LTPP) and according 'in principle' approval for each capital acquisition programme. The decisions flowing from the DAC are to be implemented by the three Boards viz the Defence Procurement Board (DPB) headed by the Defence Secretary; Defence Production Board headed by the Secretary, Defence Production; and Defence Research and Development Board headed by the Secretary, Defence Research and Development (R&D). These boards have been entrusted with specific functions. A Defence Acquisition Wing (DAW) headed by a Director General (Acquisition) was created to assist the DPB in its functioning. The new structures are intended to facilitate expeditious decision-making in an integrated manner in areas relating to acquisitions for the three Services while, at the same time, imparting a higher degree of transparency and cost-effectiveness to the process of acquisition of equipment, weapons and weapon systems. The acquisition system has been discussed in detail in the subsequent chapters.

Why is it that we have not seen implementation of a slew of reforms recommended in the last five decades by various committees on national security reforms in their reports spanning 50 years, starting with the Henderson Brooks Report of 1962 to the Naresh Chandra Committee Report of 2012? Perusal of some important and relevant recommendations shall reveal that a substantial amount of analysis in the field of acquisition has been carried out by these committees. Certain recommendations which find mention in most of these reports are as under:

Table 1.1: Recommendation of Reform Committee Reports

Committee / Report	Areas Addressed	Broad Recommendations
Group of Ministers Report, 2001[34] (as a follow-up of the Kargil Review Committee Report).	Management of defence. This report focussed on three key aspects with respect to the defence industry and self-reliance, long-term planning and coordination among various stakeholders,	The report recommended formulation of: • The Defence Ministers Council on Production (DMCP) for formulation of long-term equipment policies. The council would consist of the Raksha Mantri, Service Chiefs, Defence Secretary, Secretary Defence Departments of Space, Atomic Energy and Science and Technology were also to be

Committee / Report	Areas Addressed	Broad Recommendations
	efficiency of defence research and development and entry of the private sector in the defence industry.	members of this council, along with eminent industrialists. A separate Directorate of Planning and Coordination was also recommended to be established in the Department of Defence Production which would also function as the Secretariat for the DMCP.
		• The report recommended simplification of procedures for facilitating the participation of domestic industry in the defence sector. It made out a strong case for providing a level playing field to the private sector and an immediate rationalisation of the defence export policy. • The report also recommended collaborative R&D ventures with the private sector to be institutionalised to make R&D more result oriented and competitive. It was of the opinion that the Defence Research and Development Organisation (DRDO) should only focus on core technologies in which expertise is neither available within the country nor can be procured from alternative sources.

Committee / Report	Areas Addressed	Broad Recommendations
Kelkar Committee Report, 2005[35].	• Measures for participation of the Indian industry in the defence procurement process. • To harmonise the interests of the armed forces, Ministry of Defence, and the industry (both public and private) to increase defence exports, and to include offset provisions. • To strengthen the Ordnance Factories (OFs) and DPSUs to assume the role of system integrator.	• The Kelkar Committee submitted its report in two parts: Part One titled "Towards Strengthening Self-Reliance in Defence Preparedness" and Part Two titled "Revitalising Defence Public Sector Undertakings and Ordnance Factories". These reports contained more than fifty recommendations, the major ones of which are reproduced as follows: • Preparation of a 15-year long-term perspective plan and sharing it with the private industry. • To accord Raksha Udyog Ratna status to major players from the private sector. • Policy framework to promote the participation of small and medium enterprises in defence production. • Setting up of a dedicated and professional agency to undertake defence acquisition on the lines of the French *Direction Générale de l'Armement.* • Corporatisation of OFs on the lines of Bharat Sanchar Nigam Limited (BSNL). • Hindustan Aeronautics Limited (HAL) and Bharat Electronics Limited (BHEL) should be given Navratna status. • Certain DPSUs to be allowed to invest in foreign companies and look for mergers and acquisitions.

Committee / Report	Areas Addressed	Broad Recommendations
Sisodia Committee Report, 2007.	• Structures and procedures for defence acquisition. • Enhancing the participation of domestic defence industry in the procurement process.	• Involvement of the domestic defence industry in the acquisition process from its earliest stage for achieving self-reliance. • Long-Term Defence Capability Plan to be jointly finalised by the defence planners and the private industry. • Public version of the capability plan to be shared with the wider industry as also the defence and scientific communities. • GSQRs for major weapon systems need be jointly formulated by the Service Headquarters and the domestic arms industry for greater self-reliance. • The "Department of Defence Production" should be redesignated as the "Department of Defence Industry" with a major private sector stake under the present Additional Secretary. • The Ministry of Defence needs to issue a"Defence Industry Policy Statement" periodically clarifying the government's intent to nurture the domestic industry on the lines of the advanced countries such as the United Kingdom and Australia. • The Ministry of Defence should articulate a long-term defence export strategy in consultation with the private industry.

Committee / Report	Areas Addressed	Broad Recommendations
Rama Rao Committee Report, 2008[36].	Review of DRDO's structure with a view to improve its functioning.	• Creation of a Defence Technology Commission. • Rationalisation of DRDO laboratories. • Creation of a Board of Research for Advance Defence Sciences (BRADS) on the lines of the United States' Defence Advanced Research Projects Agency (DARPA).
Defence Expenditure Review Committee under VK Misra, 2009[37].	Curbing of wasteful defence expenditure.	• The private sector should be encouraged to become a Tier -1 player in defence production and the government should offer help by way of sovereign funds to take over foreign defence firms. • Foreign Direct Investment (FDI) in defence should be increased to 49 percent across the board and 74 to100 percent on a case to case basis. • Time-bound disinvestment plan to be worked out for each DPSU to promote transparency, accountability and efficiency. • Extensive use of information and communication technology to be made in the field of defence acquisition to compress the acquisition timelines. • Need for synergy among the DRDO, Ordnance Factory Board (OFB), DPSUs and the private sector to address design, manufacturing and maintenance concerns of India's defence.

Committee / Report	Areas Addressed	Broad Recommendations
		• The Rama Rao Committee Report should be immediately accepted.
Naresh Chandra Committee Report, 2012[38].	Reforms in national security management and higher defence management.	Appointment of a four-star permanent Chairman, Chief of Staff Committee, was one of the principal recommendations of this committee. The recommendations were incremental in nature rather than revolutionary and pertained more to structural reforms rather than purely focussing on acquisition. A major recommendation pertaining to acquisition was the setting up of the Advanced Projects Agency (APA) to undertake high-risk futuristic military research under the Scientific Adviser to the Raksha Mantri on the lines of the United States' DARPA. Enhancing FDI in defence to 49 percent and cross-postings of Ministry of Defence staff into Service Headquarters and vice versa were also recommended.
Ravinder Gupta Committee Report, 2012[39].	Modernisation of armed forces, acquisition reforms.	• Formulation of a separate Capability Development Executive for formulation of GSQRs. • Rationalisation of the trials procedure. • Professional training for acquisition staff. • Recommendations on modalities for blacklisting of companies and single vendor situation,

Committee / Report	Areas Addressed	Broad Recommendations
		• Ordnance Factory Board to be reconstituted as a holding company, disinvestment of DPSUs. • Constitution of a Defence Technology Commission on the lines of the Atomic Energy Commission (AEC) and Indian Space Research Organisation (ISRO). • Enhancement of FDI to 49 percent across the board for the manufacturing sector and 100 percent for the service sector. • Rationalising of the defence exports policy and setting of a Defence Exports Council.
Dhirendra Singh Committee Report, 2015	Revision of DPP, 2013 and laying down a policy framework for **'Make in India'**.	**Strategic Partnership model** recommended for creating capacity in the private sector on a long-term basis. Such a capacity will be created over and above the capacity and infrastructure that exists in PSUs.
		Transfer of Technology: Eligibility criteria for the selection of a production agency from amongst private Indian industry to receive Transfer of Technology (ToT) in the case of 'Buy' and 'Make' category schemes and Indian entity to receive ToT for maintenance in the case of 'Buy(Global)' category schemes need to be devised and promulgated.

Committee / Report	Areas Addressed	Broad Recommendations
		Level Playing Field: The DPP may be reviewed to facilitate and incentivise private industry, including Micro, Small and Medium Enterprises (MSMEs) to move towards 'Make in India'. Likewise, modifications would be required in other policies such as skill development and exports policy. The Indian private industry has highlighted various factors that impact competitiveness as compared to DPSUs, foreign Original Equipment Manufacturers (OEMs) and other sectors. There is, thus, a need to review such related policies to provide a level playing field and encourage participation by private industry and MSMEs; and they should be provided access to all government facilities.
		A single window system for clearance of project proposals in the defence sector to meet 'Buy (Indian)' and 'Buy and Make (Indian)' regulatory and compliance requirements for commencement of business operations should be created.
		Roadmap for Indian Defence Industry: In addition to laying down the defence production policy, the MoD should also promulgate a ten-year roadmap for the Indian defence industry, with measurable targets, in terms of revenue as percentage of defence capital expenditure as well as in terms of indigenous content value.

Committee / Report	Areas Addressed	Broad Recommendations
		Acquisition Organisation: Steps to be initiated to set up a specialised defence acquisition structure outside the formal structure of the Ministry of Defence. In the interim, the Acquisition Wing may be augmented with the JS (ICT, Policy and Tri-Services). The Department of Defence Production needs to more proactively engage with Indian private industry, just as it does with the OFB and DPSUs.
		Building the Acquisition Work Force: A tiered system of educating the acquisition work force to be evolved by HQ IDS and implemented after due approval by the MoD.
		OFB: The corporatisation of the OFB should be seen in the context of the 'Make in India' policy with its emphasis on a level playing field.
		Merger of Shipyards: The four shipyards within the MoD fold to be merged into one corporate entity, retaining the yard facilities in their present geographical locations but working under one single management.
		DRDO Export Arm: A proposal for setting up a commercial arm on the lines of the Antrix Corporation of ISRO, for providing different services including exports must be considered.

Committee / Report	Areas Addressed	Broad Recommendations
Aatre Committee Report, 2016[40]	Set up on the recommendations of the Dhirendra Singh Committee recommendations, to lay down criteria for selecting one private "strategic partner" for each of six "strategic segments" of aircraft / helicopters, warships / submarines, armoured vehicles, missiles, command and control systems, and critical materials.	The committee has recommended strategic partners in two groups. Group I has seven segments that include aircraft; helicopters; aero-engines; submarines; warships; guns and artillery; and armoured vehicles. The Task Force recommends that just one strategic partner be chosen for each segment. For the three segments in Group II, metallic material and alloys; non-metallic materials; and ammunition, including smart munitions, the Task Force recommends two strategic partners for each. A strategic partner must have a consolidated turnover of at least INR 4,000 crore for each of the last three financial years; and capital assets of INR 2,000 crore. The company should have grown at a minimum 5 per cent for at least three of the preceding five years. Finally, its credit rating must be equivalent to at least CRISIL/ICRA "A" (stable). The financial requirements for Group II are less stringent than those for Group I, since integration of systems is not needed for developing materials and ammunition. The Task Force stipulates that strategic partners must be "an engineering and/or a process technology company". The financial gate is INR 500 crore turnover for each of the last three financial years; and capital assets worth INR 100 crore.

Today, there is perhaps no sphere within the acquisition realm that remains unaddressed by diverse reform committees. Yet, as the situation obtains today, the acquisition process has displayed no dramatic performance, with hollowness at an all time high despite a steadily increasing defence allocation of around US$ 51 billion. **The irony is that the Indian military capability has not increased in proportion to the increase in spending**. Acquisition remains merely an exchange of a number of better types of equipment without any real increase in capability. There are incremental acquisitions, military unpreparedness and a mismatch between threats and capabilities.

It does, therefore, merit an analysis as to why these recommendations, so meticulously researched at the highest level, fall short of reaching the implementation stage. The reasons for non-implementation may be many. Firstly, it can partly be attributed to the lack of civilian expertise in defence and security matters. Today, no single agency in the country combines military, diplomatic, economic and intelligence capability into a coherent national strategy. While there is new thinking about Indian strategic and defence modernisation, there is still no framework that transcends the civil-military boundary. Coordination is, therefore, left to the Services themselves and depends a great deal on the issues or personalities and, ultimately, budgets. Acquisition today needs to be accorded the highest priority as is done in the developed world. There is, may be, a need to take a leaf out of the Bernard Gray acquisition reforms carried out by the UK in 2009 which recommend a Strategic Defence Review every year in the first session of Parliament. There is also a precedence in the case of the Indian space programme where a fledgling Department of Space in 1972 was directly reporting to the then Prime Minister Indira Gandhi to prevent interference by interests inimical to India.

Notes

1. "DAC Cleares Rs 11K Crore Worth Proposals", PTI, October 29, 2015, http://indiatoday.intoday.in/story/dac-cleares-rs-11k-crore-worth-proposals/1/510719.html
2. Rajat Pandit, "Indian Army Grapples with Arms, Gear Shortage", TNN, *The Times of India*, February 28, 2016, http://timesofindia.indiatimes.com/india/Indian-Army-grapples-with-arms-gear-shortage/articleshow/51173589.cms
3. Vivek Raghuvanshi, "Indian Budget Shows 10% Drop in Dollar Terms", *Defense News*, February 29, 2016, http://www.defensenews.com/ story/defense/policy-budget/budget / 2016/02/29 /indian-budget-shows-10-drop-dollar-terms/81121820/
4. Nitin Pai, "How to Buy a Rifle", *Business Standard*, July 05, 2015, http://www.business-standard.com/ article/ opinion / nitin -pai- how-to-buy-a-rifle-115070500661_1.html,.
5. Rajat Pandit, TNN | November 11, 2015, 05.56AM IST, http://timesofindia.indiatimes.com/india/No-end-to-jawans-wait-for-1-86L-bullet-proof-jackets/articleshow/49743308.cms .
6. Ajai Shukla, "'Make in India' Challenge for Kamov Helicopter", *Business Standard*, January 18, 2016, http://www.business-standard.com/article/economy-policy/make-in-india-challenge-for-kamov-helicopter-116011800029_1.html
7. DIIA Conclave, "Self-Reliance in Defence Through Design & Development", March 04, 2016, http:// bharatshakti.in /diia-conclave-self-reliance-in-defence-through-design-development/
8. Pranav Kulkarni, "Defence Procurement: Offset Threshold Raised from Rs 300 cr to Rs 2k cr, says Parrikar", *Indian Express*, February 12, 2016. http://indianexpress.com/article/business/business-others/defence-procurement-offset-threshold-raised-from-rs-300-crore-to-rs-2000-crore/#sthash.aFZQvDeo.dpuf
9. Highlights of the DAC meet on January 11, 2016, chaired by Hon'ble Defence Minister Manohar Parrikar, January 12, 2016, http://bharatshakti.in/highlights-of-the-dac-meet-on-11-jan-2016-chaired-by-honble-defence-minister-manohar-parrikar/
10. "Committee of Experts for Amendment to DPP-2013 Including Formulation of Policy Framework", http://www.mod.nic.in/ writereaddata/ Reportddp.pdf.

11. "PM Narendra Modi Addresses Combined Commanders' Conference on Board the INS *Vikramaditya*". See more at: http://indianexpress.com/article/india/india-news-india/pm-modi-addresses-combined-commanders-conference-onboard-ins-vikramaditya/#sthash.Ggtw5r0l.dpuf
12. Press Information Bureau, Prime Minister's Office "PM, Chairs Combined Commanders Conference on Board INS *Vikramaditya* at Sea", December 15, 2015, http://pib.nic.in/newsite/PrintRelease.aspx?relid=133265
13. Suhasini Haider, "As Sparring Worsens, NSA Talks are off", *The Hindu*, August 22, 2015, http://www.thehindu.com /news/international/south-asia/indiapakistan-national-security-advisorlevel-talks-called-off/article7569679.ece
14. "Pakistan Army Chief Warns India of 'Unbearable Cost of War", September 08, 2015, http://indianexpress.com/article/world/neighbours/pakistan-army-chief-raheel-sharif-warns-india-of-unbearable-cost-in-case-of-war/
15. "After China Blocks Move to Ban Masood Azhar, India Says it is Incomprehensible", PTI, *Indian Express*, April 02, 2016, http://indianexpress.com /article /india/india-news-india/india-disappointed-over-technical-hold-on-slapping-sanctions-on-pathankot-attack-mastermind-masood-azhar/,
16. "Russia-Pakistan Defence Ties Discomfit India", *The Times of India*, September 01, 2015, http://timesofindia.indiatimes. com/ india/ Russia- Pakistan-defence-ties-discomfit-India/articleshow/48752245.cms
17. Claude Arpi, "A Budget Cut That Has Unsettled The PLA", *The Pioneer*, March 13, 2016, http://www.dailypioneer.com/columnists/edit/a-budget-cut-that-has-unsettled-the-pla.html
18. n. 15.
19. Anjana Pasricha, "India Rejects Joint Naval Patrols with US in South China Sea", Voice of America (VoA), March 11, 2016, http://www. voanews.com / content/ india-rejects-joint-naval-patrols-with-us-in-south-china-sea/3231567.html
20. "Know Your Own Strength", http://www.economist.com/news/briefing/21574458-india-poised-become-one-four-largest-military-powers-world-end, *The Economist*, March 30, 2013
21. Rajat Pandit, "India Remains World's Largest Arms Importer", March 17, 2015, http://timesofindia.indiatimes.com/india/India-remains-worlds-largest-arms-importer/articleshow/46591086.cms
22. "Face-off in Ladakh as PLA Erects Watchtower", *The Times of India,* September 13, 2015. http://timesofindia.indiatimes.com/india/Face-off-in-Ladakh-as-PLA-erects-watchtower/articleshow/48940404.cms

23. n. 15.
24. Sushant Singh, "Nukes Are Not For War", *Indian Express*, December 25, 2015, http://indianexpress.com/article/opinion/columns/india-shouldnt-abandon-its-nuclear-doctrine-because-of-pakistans-tactical-nukes/
25. Sudhi Ranjan Sen, "India's Nuclear Triad in Sight as INS *Arihant* Prepares for First Missile Test", NDTV News, July 11, 2015, http://www.ndtv.com/india-news/indias-nuclear-triad-in-sights-as-ins-arihant-preps-for-first-missile-test-780415
26. Smita Gupta, "Army Chief's Leaked Letter to PM puts Centre in a Fix", *The Hindu*, March 28, 2012, http://www.thehindu.com/news/national/army-chiefs-leaked-letter-to-pm-puts-centre-in-a-fix/article3255243.ece
27. Laxman Kumar Behera, "Why India's Defence Preparedness is Hollow", Rediff News, April 02, 2012, http://www.rediff.com/ news/column/why-indias-defence-preparedness-is-hollow-column/20120402.htm
28. Shishir Gupta, "Govt Set to Give Permanent Status to Top Post in Indian Military", *Hindustan Times*, April 10, 2016, http://www. hindustantimes. com/ india/govt-set-to-give-permanent-status-to-top-post-in-indian-military/story-SyxAjQLArssn LehD0LQUsN.html
29. Pandit, n. 2.
30. Gupta, n.26.
31. Lt Gen PC Katoch, "Defence Budget: Surrendering Funds has put Brakes on India's Military Modernization", *First Post India*, March 07, 2016, http://www.firstpost.com/india/defence-budget-surrendering-funds-has-put-brakes-on-indias-military-modernisation-2660566.html
32. Ajai Shulka, "CAG Criticises Army`s Purchase Procedures", May 19, 2007, http://ajaishukla. blogspot.in /2007_05_01_ archive.html
33. Kanishka Singh, "Parrikar Eases Defence Blacklisting Policy, *Sunday Guardian*, February 27, 2016, http://www.sunday guardian live.com/news/3511-parrikar-eases-defence-blacklisting-policy
34. "GoM Report on National Security Management, Appointment, Approach & Methodology", http://www.vifindia.org /sites/default/files/GoM%20Report%20on% 20National % 20Security.pdf
35. "Kelkar Committee Submits Report on Defence Acquisition", http://www.geod.in/wp-content/uploads /2015/ 03/ Kelkar - Committee-submits-report-on-defence-acquisition.pdf
36. "Rama Rao Committee on DRDO", *CG Staff News*, February 21, 2010, http://cgstaffnews.com/?p=639

37. "Defence Expenditure Review Committee (DERC) Panel Proposals" http:// indiandefenceindustry. blogspot. in/2009/12/ defence-expenditure-review-committee.html
38. Anit Mukherjee, "Marching Forward on Reform", *The Hindu*, June 17, 2012, http://www.thehindu.com/opinion/op-ed/marching-forward-on-reform/article3646651.ece
39. RS Chauhan, "Defence Procurement to be Made more Transparent", *Rediff News,* March 11, 2013, http://www.rediff.com /news/report/defence-procurement-to-be-made-more-transparent/20130311.htm
40. Ajai Shukla, "Aatre Task Force Recommends Rs 4,000 Crore Entry Bar for Private Firms Building Weaponry as 'Strategic Partners'", http://ajaishukla.blogspot.in/2016/01/rs-4k-cr-entry-bar-for-pvt-firms.html

2. OVERVIEW OF DEFENCE CAPITAL ACQUISITION SYSTEM

Modernisation of the Armed forces is incumbent upon acquisition of weapon systems and platforms from indigenous and foreign sources. Defence procurement is carried out as per the provisions of the DPP and flows from the capability required by the Services to meet the national security imperatives. All proposals for capability development and subsequent acquisitions flow from the defence planning process which covers the long, medium and short terms' perspectives. Essentially, the planning process for acquisition is initiated by the issue of the Raksha Mantri's (RM's) Operational Directive from which flow the 15-year Long-Term Integrated Perspective Plan (LTIPP) for the defence forces, the five-year Services Capital Acquisition Plan (SCAP) and Annual Acquisition Plan (AAP), which is, in essence, a two-year roll-on plan for capital acquisition. HQ IDS, in consultation with the SHQ, prepares the LTIPP, SCAP, and AAP jointly for the three Services. Over the years, the defence acquisition organisation of the country too has matured. A functional mechanism has evolved wherein, from the planning stage to final contract implementation, the three Services and HQ IDS, on the one hand, and the MoD with its Finance, Technical and Acquisition Wings, on the other, work in unison through the institutions of the Services Capital Acquisition Plan Categorisation Committee (SCAPCC), Services Capital Acquisition Plan Categorisation Higher Committee, (SCAPCHC), DPB and DAC. Therein lies a problem: to balance the urgent need for modernisation of the defence forces of the country with the protracted process of decision-making.

The formalised acquisition procedure of arms and equipment through the capital route has been promulgated fairly recently in India. The Public Accounts Committee of Parliament, in its 187th Report in 1989, recommended that the government should formulate comprehensive guidelines relating to defence purchases and contracts. Accordingly, the guidelines to this effect that were issued in 1992, sought to address these concerns. They embraced the concept of a Long-Term Perspective Plan (LTPP), the Services' five-year capital acquisition plan and 'Make' and 'Buy' decisions. The process continued when, in the aftermath of the Kargil War, the higher defence management was subjected to a scrutiny by a GoM and comprehensive reforms in the defence acquisition institutional and procedural set-up were ushered in. The guiding principles for these reforms were jointness, synergy, building up of expertise, and collegiate decision-making. All these were to be achieved by establishing institutional mechanisms at various levels.

The findings of the Kargil Review Committee (KRC) brought to the fore many grave deficiencies in India's national security management. The committee observed that national security management recedes into the background in times of peace and is considered too delicate to be tampered with in times of war. The continuing proxy war and the prevailing nuclearised security environment justify a thorough review of the national system in its entirety. Realising the fact that such a review cannot be undertaken by an overburdened bureaucracy, an independent body of credible experts – a national commission of one or more task forces – was recommended to be constituted to undertake studies on specific issues set out below. It is important to understand the rationale of the committee's approach to the long overdue review and resolution of the national security problems. The committee recommended a need to reorganise the entire gamut of national security management and apex decision-making structure. The committee stressed for the establishment of a full-time National Security Adviser (NSA) who would be backed by a full time permanent secretariat and strategic and technical intelligence and would brief the Cabinet Committee on Security (CCS) from time to time. The committee also recommended that a Defence Intelligence Agency (DIA) be set up to coordinate the intelligence collection and analysis effort of the three Services. The committee also acknowledged an urgent need to enhance the financial outlay for defence to enable modernisation and a need to build a relationship between DRDO and the defence Services to enable credible and mutually beneficial R&D programmes. As a follow-up of the KRC, a separate task force on "Management of Defence" was set up. This report focussed on three key aspects with reference to the defence industry and self-reliance: long-term planning and coordination among various stakeholders, efficiency of DRDO, and entry of the private sector in the defence industry. The report recommended establishment of the Defence Ministers Council on Production (DMCP) for the formulation of long-term equipment policies. The council would consist of the RM, Service Chiefs, Defence Secretary, Secretary (DP), Scientific Adviser (SA) to the Raksha Mantri, Chief of the Integrated Staff Committee (CISC) and Financial Adviser Defence Services (FADS). Secretaries of the Departments of Space, Atomic Energy and Science and Technology were also to be members of this council, along with eminent industrialists. A separate Directorate of Planning and Coordination was also recommended to be established in the Department of Defence Production(DDP) which would also function as the Secretariat for the DMCP. The report recommended simplification of procedures for facilitating the participation of domestic industry in the defence sector. It made out a strong case for providing a level playing field to the private sector and an immediate rationalisation of the defence export policy. The report also recommended collaborative R&D ventures with the private sector to be institutionalised to make R&D more result oriented and competitive. It was of the opinion that DRDO should only focus on core technologies in which expertise is neither available within the country nor can be procured from alternative sources. The KRC was a precursor to the establishment of the DG (Director General) Acquisition and a detailed version of the DPP.

As mentioned above, the DPP as a procedure for defence procurement was initially formalised in 1992, as laid down vide

MoD ID No1 (1)/91/PO (Def) dated February 28, 1992. Based on the recommendations of the GoM on reforming the national security system, the experience gained, and the feedback from the industry, the original DPP went through continuous modifications. Subsequently, the first DPP came into effect on December 30, 2002. Thereafter, the first manual of the procurement procedure for capital acquisitions, namely, DPP 2005, was issued and incorporated suggestions received from the Chief Vigilance Commissioner (CVC) and Comptroller and Auditor General (C & AG). DPP 2006 incorporated the revised the "Fast Track Procedure" (FTP) and Procedure for Indigenous Warship-Building. In addition, a major addition in this volume was the 'Make' procedure, which provided the requisite framework for increased participation of Indian industry; the 'Integrity Pact' for contracts above Rs 100 crore and 'offsets' obligations for contracts in excess of Rs 300 crore. Also, the recommendations of the Parliamentary Standing Committee on Defence and the Kelkar Committee were relied upon during the review. DPP 2008 (Amendment 2009) primarily focussed on promoting the indigenous defence industry; and providing transparency and integrity in all acquisitions. In addition, a new category for acquisition, 'Buy and Make (Indian)' was introduced. Subsequently, DPP 2011 was further refined based on experience gained and inputs from foreign and Indian industry. In addition, the Ship-Building Procedure was revised comprehensively to encourage private participation and the offset policy guidelines were expanded considerably. The review of DPP 2011 was completed through a built-in mechanism in the document and the same has been revised to DPP 2016.

DPP 2016, promulgated with effect from March 28, 2016, is the latest version. Some of the salient amendments which have been effected in this version are: *firstly*, the preferred order of categorisation has been introduced with Indigenously Designed Developed and Manufactured (IDDM) as the first priority and 'Buy Global' as the last priority. *Secondly*, the validity of the AoN has been reduced to six months from the existing one year, except for 'Buy and Make (Indian)' cases. *Thirdly*, cogent means have been introduced to encourage the private sector's participation. Efforts have also been made to address key areas of the GSQRs and field evaluation trials to make them simpler and more effective.

DPP 2016 has as its basis an exhaustive seven-chapter report of an experts committee[1] chaired by Dhirendra Singh, a former DG (Acquisition),which has attempted to put the overall gamut of capital acquisition in perspective. The committee included members from all the key stakeholder institutions: the armed forces, various wings of the MoD Department of Defence Production (DDP), Department of Defence (DoD), DRDO, and the industry. The major focus of the expert committee was on streamlining the acquisition process and structure so as to create more opportunities for the local industry, including forming of strategic partnerships with them. The committee recommended that for 'Make in India' to succeed, the local industry needs to prosper, and, hence, there is a need to take it into confidence in every possible procurement step, beginning with the planning process which now forms the basis of the 'strategic partnership' which is a part of DPP 2016. Highlighting the current weakness whereby the local industry does not have information about the type and nature of the long-term equipment requirements of the armed forces, the committee has suggested that the relevant information as contained in various plans and other documents be shared with the industry with the sole objective of enabling the latter to make concrete decisions on investment or technology partnership. In specific terms, the committee has suggested the revision of the current Technology Perspective Capability Roadmap (TPCR) so as to reflect the type and nature of the equipment required by the armed forces in the next 15 years. At the same time, the committee has also suggested that schemes amenable to 'Make' projects be shared with the industry along with the details of other schemes as contained in the 5-year SCAP which too finds a mention in the latest version of the DPP.

The recommendations of DPP 2016 are bound to have a major bearing on both the Army and industry and are likely to usher in an era of transformational change. One of the important milestones of the latest DPP 2016 lies in a clear acknowledgement of the fact that defence material, when compared to civil products, has certain highly distinctive features. Defence material is highly technology intensive, dominated by multinational control regimes, costly to develop and composed of complex systems subject to rigorous trials. Pricing decisions for defence procurements are highly complex, with little or no applicability of standard market forces to these contracts. Resultantly, a military capability comprises not merely procurement of equipment but deployment of a complex man-machine mix; hence, in the words of the committee, "unwitting" comparisons between civil and military procurements should not be made. The need and importance of treating defence procurement and markets in the "same template devised for procurement of civil products," therefore, needs to be avoided. This revolutionary distinction will, in the times to come, herald a paradigm shift in the way defence acquisition is viewed in India. This also may rid the Services of the long standing delays caused by instances such as single vendor situations created due to the inability of stakeholders to fathom this vital distinction between military and civilian procurements. Further, on the lines of a Strategic Defence Review (SDR) recommended by the Bernard Gray acquisition reforms of 2009[2] in the UK, the committee has recommended that a national consensus be developed to generate military power in India.

In the past, a number of committees on acquisition reforms, primarily the Kelkar Committee, talked about the establishment of an enhanced procurement organisation modelled on the Direction Générale de l'Armement (DGA) of France. On the same lines, the Dhirendra Singh Committee has reiterated the recommendation of a proactive defence procurement executive, with specialist wings and personnel working outside the confines of a staff oriented environment of the government establishment in order to spearhead the procurement process, and, at the same time, working seamlessly with the MoD and SHQ. In a shift from the traditional stance, the committee also stresses that "hand-holding and nurturing" would be the DNA of such procurement executive rather than a "hands-off" approach where meetings with industry personnel are looked upon with suspicion, and are discouraged. This recommendation in itself may well be the beginning of a state-of-the-art acquisition organisation in India on the lines of the DGA of France or the Australian Defence Material Organisation (DMO). The DPP is, however, silent in this regard.

Several structural and procedural recommendations to the DPP are on the anvil which have immense potential of simplifying the existing acquisition process as also reducing the acquisition timelines, in keeping with international best practices, where significant time and resources are devoted towards streamlining an acquisition business case before the Request for Proposal (RFP) is floated. Certain 'pre RFP' recommendations have been made by the committee to include making the Technology Perspective Capability Roadmap (TPCR) more specific as also fielding the five-year Services Capital Acquisition Plan (SCAP) and 'Make' projects in the public domain in order to provide a more accurate direction to the private industry of the perspective requirements of the Services. The Request for Information (RFI) function will now be a "structured interaction" with the Indian industry rather than a one-way document. The defence acquisitions do not follow the dynamics of commercial markets: the 'capability' sought by the Services should not be negotiated in favour of 'best price,' therefore, every single vendor situation, even at the *ab-initio* SQR stage, should not always be construed as unacceptable. Based on this logic, minor deviations from SQRs at the technical or field evaluation stages, need to be accepted, to avoid setting the acquisition clock back by many years. Similarly, even in a single vendor situation, post technical evaluation by the Technical Evaluation Committee (TEC), retraction of the RFP may be resorted to only as an exception rather than a rule in case a re-tendering is unlikely to increase the vendor base. The DPP 2016 also contains a provision of doing away with the mandatory 'approval' of the TEC undertaken by SHQ from DG Acquisition for those delegated under the powers of the SHQ, which was a major delay factor. The area of field evaluation trials has been identified as one of the most critical delay factors in the acquisition chain, however, the committee is of the view that a major initiative to optimise the field trial process, perhaps in terms of a 'joint single trial,' should actually come from the Services themselves and the acquisition set-up should facilitate such initiatives. The approval of the 'Staff Evaluation Report' shall now be done in SHQ at the Vice Chief level, on the same lines as recommended for the TEC report. Constitution of a Commercial Negotiation Committee (CNC), similarly, has been recommended to be de-linked with the acceptance of the Technical Oversight Committee (TOC) report. The CNC can now be constituted on acceptance of the 'Staff Evaluation Report', with the caveat that opening of commercial bids and negotiations with the vendor would not be done till the acceptance of the TOC report by the concerned Competent Financial Authority (CFA). Regrettably, in the case of commercial bid evaluation criteria, the committee has, while accepting models such as Life Cycle Costing (LCC), Performance-Based Logistics (PBL), Total Cost of Acquisition (TCA) and L1T1 (L1 – Lowest Cost – T1 – Technical) accorded primacy to the existing L1 system with certain modifications. This may deprive the Services of the advantages offered by the state-of-the-art evaluation criteria such as Quality-cum-Cost-Based Systems (QCBS) and 'Cost Performance Trade-Off' systems in vogue in more advanced Armies the world over. DPP 2016 will be based on the recommendations of this committee to the extent of its implementation.

Make in India

It is imperative that any overview of the acquisition system must factor in the current level of progress of the government's 'Make in India' campaign. At the policy level, DPP 2016 ushers in a policy framework for 'Make in India' recommended by the experts committee. The global manufacturing sector has been witnessing a major change in the present times. The cost factor is becoming more and more important, forcing manufacturers the world over to decide on new locations for sourcing and manufacturing of their products. India's performance on cost competitiveness as per the Boston Consulting Group (BCG) manufacture cost competitiveness index 2016, is constrained by issues of infrastructure and poor governance. Also, India has held steady over the years in terms of relative costs, unlike China which has lost its cost competitiveness. India, however, does moderately well in the infrastructure sector but loses out badly in ease of doing business where it ranks 142 out of 175 responses while China is at 90th position, Thailand at 26 and the US at 7. In terms of overall business environment, India ranks 57 while China is at 50. In terms of logistics performance, India is at 54 while China is at 28; and in corruption perception, India has recently improved its position to 76 as per the latest transparency index figures released by Transparency International in 2015[3].

Post the announcement of 'Make in India', the global armament majors once again have India on their radars. In the past, they were more inclined to enter the Indian defence market through direct sales to the world's largest arms importer. But this time, they are endorsing the 'Make in India' slogan to be in perfect tune with the new government. As many as 330 foreign companies participated in the Aero-India Show held in February 2015 in Bangalore, with another 270 Indian companies also marking their presence at the five-day exhibition, which was inaugurated by Prime Minister Narendra Modi. The ninth Def Expo held at Goa in the last week of March 2016 attracted 490 foreign and 540 Indian companies which displayed their collective might at the mega event.[4]

The biennial Aero-India, ongoing since 1996, has become a major platform for armament giants over the last decade, with India's emergence as the world largest arms importer, inking, as it has, defence deals worth well over $60 billion[5]. Six months later, as things stand today, India has received investment proposals of over INR 1,10,000 crore or US$ 17 billion from various companies for all the sectors put together. The change can be gauged from the fact that about 25 per cent smart phones shipped in the country in the April to June quarter were made in India.

Maintaining the cost advantage, the Indian manufacturing sector would need to keep a check on increase in wages and other factor costs which may still be achievable. The difficult part is to address the non-cost factors i.e. improve poor infrastructure, radicalise labour reforms, put in place simpler tax structures and provide easier access to the credit mechanism. Also, India will have to show a dramatic improvement in ease of doing business which is the most difficult part. DPP 2016, once fully implemented, is expected to put in place a policy, creating a single window clearance mechanism for at least the defence projects which in itself is a forward step. As per the report, in India, the business operations in the defence sector are conducted either through licensed production, sub-contracting, Joint Ventures (JVs) or foreign technology collaboration agreements, apart from local start-ups. A number of agencies are involved in this process. Norms for JVs are issued by the Department of Industrial Policy and Promotion (DIPP), Foreign Direct Investment (FDI) matters are handled by the Foreign Investment Promotion Board (FIPB), foreign technology collaboration agreements are dealt with by the Reserve Bank of India (RBI), sub-contracting matters are subject to advance licensing, excise and customs law. A single window system within the MoD for clearance of project proposals in the defence sector to meet 'Buy (Indian)' and 'Buy and Make (Indian)' regulatory and compliance requirements for commencement of business operations will be created through DPP 2016. Even after the establishment of such a system, operational issues needing interaction with diverse agencies and ministries viz Ministry of Commerce (MoC) for licensing issues, Ministry of Home Affairs (MHA) for security clearances, Ministry of Finance (MoF) for equity matters, Directorate General of Foreign Trade (DGFT) for exports and imports, and Ministry of External Affairs (MEA) for export controls, etc will require coordination. This is intended to be facilitated through an internal mechanism in the DDP. India has set for itself a target of enhancing the share of manufacturing to 25 percent of the Gross Domestic Product (GDP) to INR 25.6 trillion and creating 1,00,000 manufacturing jobs within a decade. The growth target for manufacture has been set at 10 percent per annum, however, the present growth rate is only three percent per annum and, resultantly, several sectors where there is a robust domestic demand, are still dependant on imports. These are electronics, defence and aerospace which have benefitted by easing of the regulations. There is a tendency of global supply chains to offshore low risk items to suitable manufacturing destinations of which india can take advantage too. However, sectors such as textiles, auto components, electronics, chemicals, and, finally, defence and aerospace can drive the government's 'Make in India' plan.

Among the 25 sectors identified for the 'Make in India' campaign, defence and aerospace are being looked upon as among the most promising sectors to promote indigenous manufacturing. The defence sector is most amenable to 'Make in India', due to the captive market and, hence, global players should be willing to invest in India. The low manufacturing cost and the size of the market are the biggest advantages. Easing of the regulatory framework too has its attractions for the defence industry. Easing of FDI norms to 49 percent, permitting Foreign Institutional Investment (FII) portfolio investments through the automatic route[6] and clearing pending proposals due to a policy shift, which allows an Indian company to hold a cumulative share of 51 percent, has energised the JVs. Earlier, only a single Indian company had to own and control the entire JV. Over the next seven years, the government is planning to spend US$ 130 billion on defence and US$ 110 billion on homeland security. The Indian defence and aerospace market is the seventh largest globally, with a strong domestic demand. The DAC has categorised sourcing of an unprecedented approximately INR two lakh crore in the past almost one year plus. These initiatives, like increase in the FDI limit is resulting in JVs and ToT, and product development in India. However, the industry feels that 49 percent FDI is not adequate[7]. The government has also de-licensed a large number of defence products and the 'Make' procedure is under review with the first order of Battlefield Management System (BMS) being given to the ROLTA and Bharat Eectronics Limited (BHEL) consortium. To encourage 'Make in India' in defence, there is a need to leverage the strength of Small and Medium Enterprises (MSMEs), create skill sets, as well as acquisition of foreign companies abroad.

The private industry has responded with enthusiasm to the 'Make in India' initiative. To quote a few examples, OIS Advanced Technology (AT), which is already the OEM for India for advanced Air Defence (AD) systems, plans to manufacture the L 70 AD gun and close-in weapon system for the Indian Army. It also plans to carry out Pichora upgrades for the Indian Air Force (IAF) in collaboration with a number of North Atlantic Treaty Organisation (NATO) countries. Under the 'Make in India' initiative, OIS proposes to establish a manufacturing facility in India by Financial Year (FY) 2015-16 itself. Initial investment in excess of INR 500 crore by OIS AT and its consortium partners will include gun systems, radar systems and their components. The OIS group also has one of the six Indian licences for the manufacture of mini and micro Unmanned Aerial Vehicles (UAVs). OIS has formed key partnerships and alliances wih growing manufacture companies for nurturing its manufacture programme. The company is gearing up for a global launch of four advanced technologies dual use radar systems. BAE Systems is partnering with Hindustan Aeronautics Limited (HAL) where the Hawk trainer aircraft is being assembled to continue the development of its training, performance, and operational capabilities. It is also partnering with HAL to develop the Tactical Communication System (TCS) and working on the development of a Precision Guided Munition (PGM) rocket for fixed wing and rotary wing platforms. Boeing is also in talks with Indian companies for the manufacture of spare parts for the Chinook and Apache helicopters. Safran has a legacy of 60 years in India in the three core business areas of aerospace, defence and security. It has formed a JV with HAL for the manufacture of engines for the Mirage 2000, Jaguars and Hawk trainers. It is also supplying engines for the Indian built 'Dhruv' helicopters, and for the Light Combat Helicopter (LCH) and Light Utility Helicopter (LUH) programmes of HAL. It is also providing inertial navigation systems, optronics and flight controls developed in-house. Safran is also involved in R&D in India with collaborative arrays with the Indian Institute of Technology (IIT), Delhi, and Indian Institute of Science (IISc), Bengaluru. Russia too intends to share new technology with India to include the Ka 226 T offset programme. Russia intends to manufacture the Ka 226 T in India with the fuselage and main rotor to be made in India while the final product is also intended to be assembled in India for domestic consumption and subsequent exports. The Komov Ka 226 T was a forerunner in the contract for 197 LUH along with Airbus which was later cancelled after seven years of negotiations in 2014. The Komov offset programme on offer by Russia would include establishment of a training centre for pilots. In August 2015, moving ahead on this INR 6,000 crore 'Make in India' project for military helicopters, Russia has informed the MoD about a partnership with Reliance Defence to manufacture the Kamov 226T helicopters locally and has announced an understanding with the subsidiary company of Reliance Infrastructure as a lead integrator for the mega contract to manufacture 200 twin-engine helicopters for the Indian Army[8]. HAL is already collaborating with the MIL Design Bureau, Moscow, to start development of the Indian multi-role helicopter which may be provided as an offset by Russia in case the contract for purchase of helicopters is concluded.

In the current Twelfth Army Five-Year Plan, 2012-17, which is in consonance with the Artillery Profile 2027, the Indian Army plans to upgrade its existing field regiments, presently equipped with the 105 mm Indian field guns, 105 mm light field guns and the Russian 122 mm guns, to the 155 mm towed gun system as a universal inventory. As per the Artillery Modernisation Plan, the Indian Army requires 814 mounted guns, 1,580 towed guns, 100 tracked self-propelled guns,180 wheeled self-propelled guns and 145 ultra light howitzers at a cost of approximately Rs one lakh crore. The 155mm / 45-calibre Dhanush howitzers had "successfully met all technical parameters" during the winter and summer trials at Sikkim and Pokhran. The RM in a recent statement to this affect made to the parliamentary committee, also stated that Dhanush incorporates "many improved features" over the Army's existing artillery guns. In addition to the Dhanush, the DRDO is also developing a 155 mm / 52 Cal Advance Towed Artillery Gun System (ATAGS) that will upgrade the 155 mm / 45 calibre Dhanush in the future. The ATAGS, a light-weight long range automated gun being developed by DRDO with private participation, will be ready for production by 2019 after undergoing six years of development and testing. Larsen and Toubro (L&T) emerged the finalist for a $750 million (about INR 5,000 crore) contract to manufacture and supply 100 self-propelled artillery guns to the Indian Army. Christened the K9 Vajra-T howitzer, pitched by L&T in partnership with Samsung, it has been shortlisted for the contract. The Vajra will be produced at L&T's Pune facility and could be considered for export in the future, along with an expected follow-on order for more guns for the Army. To its credit, L&T bagged the order after competing in the global category, which was open to all arms vendors around the world. The Vajra beat its Russian competitor on several technical grounds, including rate of fire, accuracy and mobility trials. In addition to this, the M 777 ULH deal worth US$ 700 million has been recently signed with the US through the Foreign Military Sales (FMS) route[9] and Mahindra Defence Systems has been chosen by the US as its domestic partner.

A new policy is on the anvil to revitalise 3,500 MSMEs involved in defence manufacture in a big way. Many of these MSMEs are engaged in the production of sub-systems for OEMs. The present government has created an opportunity of US$ 3 billion for the MSMEs through 'Make in India', through the new offsets policy. The MSME sector is expected to come up with a business of INR 18,000 crore which is 20 percent of the overall projection of the defence sector. The IAF projects an emerging opportunity of INR 72,000 crore, the Navy, INR 13,000 crore, and the Army, INR 4,500 crore. Defence offsets over the last few years have been worth INR 28,800 crore and the IAF has inked contracts worth INR 21,600 crore, the Navy for INR 5,064 crore and the Army for INR 144 crore. MSMEs are expected to fulfill the requirements for sub-systems and sub-assays through reverse engineering of tanks, aircraft, helicopters, submarines, ships and UAVs, Electronic Warfare (EW) suites, radar systems and optronic systems, displays, etc. Over the next 10-15 years, India will need to replace a considerable portion of its major systems and technologies to keep pace with the emerging requirements. In about the next 15 years, the import to indigenous ratio will be 50:50. DPSUs are required to source 20 percent of their annual requirements from MSMEs. Also, there are 358 items reserved for MSMEs. BHEL has set up a defence integration complex in Andhra Pradesh (AP) for establishing an ecosystem for manufacturing electronic components in collaboration with SMEs. Similarly, Tata Power has initiated building its INR 450 crore defence production unit in Karnataka.

On the World Bank global index for ease of doing business, India ranks 130th out of a study of 189 economies and has moved up from its 142 position in 2015. Bhutan ranks 77th, Nepal 89th and Sri Lanka ranks 107th in the index. India takes 29 days for starting a business on an average, while New Zealand, which is at the top rank, takes just half a day. Singapore takes 26 days to issue a construction permit, while India takes 192 days. For obtaining an electricity connection, South Korea takes 18 days, while India takes over 90.New Zealand, numero uno in registering property, takes one day; India takes 47 days. The average duration of bankruptcy proceedings in India is around 4.3 years, while in Singapore, it is just 9.5 months. India ranks 42nd for getting credit and for enforcing contracts it is 178th.On the policy front, the government presently has taken a number of initiatives with INR one billion being provided as the defence technology fund, and INR 22.5 billion for bolstering the border infrastructure. It had delicensed a large number of components and spares. The Indian government has asked its envoys in over 160 countries to focus on economic diplomacy in order to attract investments. The states have been mobilised and initiatives such as 'Make in Northeast' have been planned.

No state in India has yet developed a comprehensive list of licences, No Objection Certificates (NOCs) and registrations required to set up and operate a business. Emphasising the need to bridge the gap between implementation on paper and on the ground, a Rajya Sabha sub-committee on ease of doing business has advocated an online single-window approval mechanism with an enforceable timeline for each service, formulation of a common application form, a single post-construction completion and occupancy certificate, and auto approval based on certification of the structural design and architectural drawings by recognised engineers and architects. The committee recommends a review of all applicable forms and rules for registration of an enterprise, providing for a single application form with a single-payment gateway and a unique business ID number, incorporating all information regarding a business, to be taken as the sole reference for registration and other regulatory processes. The government must seriously introspect, scale down, simplify and reorient the structure, making it responsive in quick time to the needs of the people and the industry. The important "works in progress", as Union Finance Minister Arun Jaitley terms them, such as the GST, insolvency and bankruptcy law, amendments in the Companies Act 2013 and others, including easier tax compliance and time-definite waiver of penalty, etc, will hopefully be in place very soon[10].

The Uttar Pradesh (UP) government has secured an investment of INR 5,000 crore for manufacturing mobile sets in the state. Similarly, Maharashtra has secured an investment of INR 6,266 crore. Sony Corp is getting back to manufacturing in India after nearly a decade and plans to manufacture Bravia sets at Foxcoms' Sriperembudur plant. The Hinduja Group plans an investment of INR 5,000 crore as a part of its Headened in the Sky (HTS) technology initiative for its TV distribution business. Czech companies are looking towards investing in the automobile, energy, infrastructure and defence sectors. Seimens plans to invest US$ 1.3 billion and enhance its existing workforce from 4,000 to 16,000. Samsung Electronics has invested US$ 78 million for expansion of its manufacturing plant in NOIDA. Foxconn is planning an aggressive expansion of its manufacturing infrastructure in India by adding 12 new factories, and will employ as many as one million workers by 2020. In an effort to push the digital India initiative, Silicon valley-based tech giant Qualcomm will invest US$ 150 million for Indian start-ups. Public Private Participation (PPP) is now a new imperative. Indigenisation has been given preeminence in various policy statements from the government. It has been emphasised that the Indian public and private sectors should play a larger role to provide state-of-the-art equipment for the Indian forces. The private sector has been playing a significant role in the defence industry as a sub-contractor/ ancillary industry. It has been actively involved in the supply of raw materials, semi-finished products and certain hi-tech equipment to the tune of 25 percent to the DPSUs/ OFs. The private sector not only has the management expertise but also the resources to spend on research and technology. The world is seeing a noticeable change in the strategic landscape over the last two decades. The private sector has taken the lead to adapt to the changes in the defence sector. The opportunity is unprecedented with $ 100 billion expected to be sunk in the next 10 years. The success of 'Make in India' hinges on the success of the defence sector.

Capital Acquisition Process

Defence Planning Dimension: The capital acquisition process commences from the defence planning process. Defence planning comprises not only operational planning but also important planning for force levels, organising and equipping of the armed forces; all these aspects are inter-related and inter-dependent. Contingency operational planning apart, all defence planning has to be on a steady, long-term basis. Firstly, so that not only is the current security threat catered for, but also the foreseeable future threats and going beyond that, the desired capability is created. Secondly, to ensure that a proper balance is maintained between economic development and the capability desired. In the post-independence years, prior to 1964, defence planning was done on an annual basis. The first six-year Defence Plan was formulated in 1964. It was, however, no more than a sum total of estimated yearly budgets for the next five years. The 1969-74 Defence Plan took into account the long-term forecast of requirements of the defence system as a whole, within the framework of national resources. This was followed by the 1970-75 roll-on plan, which permitted a carry forward of fund allocations, expenditure and targets from one year to the next, within the plan period. The events of 1971, however, overtook the assumptions made and, thus, immediate imperatives had to take precedence over long-term concepts, and priorities changed. In 1973-74, a high level planning group was set up under the Minister of Planning to consider the Defence Plan 1974-79, the fundamental approach being to review the plan objectives against a high level assessment of threat and then relating them to the National Development Plan, thus, ensuring intimate complementary relations between defence and development. A high level inter-Service Defence Planning Staff (DPS) under the MoD was created in 1986 to assist the Chief of Staff Committee (COSC). It had senior inter-Service staff along with senior representatives from the MoD, MoD (Finance), MEA and a senior scientist from the DRDO. The DPS was headed by Director General Defence Planning

Staff (DG DPS), held in rotation among the three Services by an officer of the rank of Lieutenant General / equivalent. The DPS was made responsible for the preparation of coordinated perspective defence plans based on projections received from the Perspective Planning Directorates in the SHQ, DDP and DRDO. The DPS was to undertake periodic threat assessment to evolve a mix of force levels and weaponry to integrate the requirements of the three Services to meet the threat. Based on the recommendations of the GoM, the IDS was set up in 2001. The organisation of the DG DPS was merged into the IDS on the formation of HQ IDS due to which apex level planning has suffered.

Long-term plans are prepared by the HQ IDS reporting to the COSC. These form the basis for medium-term plans i.e. the SCAPs and AAPs which are the annual plans. Approval for such plans is accorded by the DAC. Emergency purchases and consideration of intricate matters are done through a collegiate decision-making process by the DPB, chaired by the Defence Secretary. The efforts of the production and research agencies are synergised with the requirements of the Services through production and R&D Boards chaired by their respective Secretaries.

Fig 2.1: Defence Planning Process

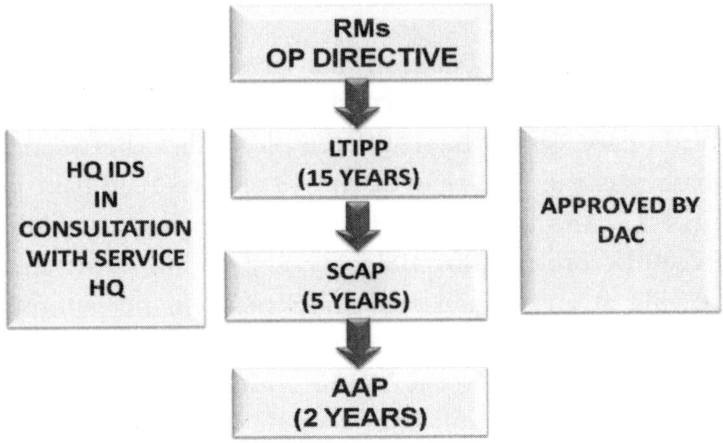

Budgetary Dimension: The budgetary allocation to the Defence Services is provided under the Defence Services Estimates (DSE) which comprise the following Demands for Grants (DFG) in the changed format, beginning 2016:

Table 2.1: Demand for Grants

(a)	DFG 20 – MoD (Misc)
(b)	DFG 21 - Defence Pensions
(c)	DFG 22 - Defence Services, Revenue
(d)	DFG 23 - Defence Services Capital

MoD Misc contains the revenue and capital expenditure of the MoD Secretariat and other organisations, such as the Armed Forces Tribunal (AFT), Coast Guard (CG), Canteen Stores Department (CSD), Defence Estates Organisation (DEO), Defence Accounts Department (DAD), etc. Plus, the entire revenue and capital budget of the DGOF and the DRDO (previously part of DSE) has been added here. It also consists of the revenue and capital expenditure of five organisations, namely, Military Farms (MFs), Ex-Servicemen Health Scheme (ECHS), Inspection Organisation (IO), Rashtriya Rifles (RR), and National Cadet Corps (NCC) which earlier used to be embedded in the DFG for the Army, and the capital budget of these organisations used to be a part of the DSE.

Striking a balance between the pressing needs of defence and other development sectors, the defence budget has grown at a steady pace, since the 1999 Kargil conflict. Between 2007-08, which was the first year of the 11th Five-Year Plan period, and 2014-15, the outlay for defence more than doubled from INR 92,000 crore in 2007-08 to INR 2,03,500 crore in 2013-14, growing at an average rate of 13 per cent per annum. The defence budget is the third largest single item of expenditure in the non-plan segment of the union budget; indeed, in some of the years, it was the second largest single item of expenditure. As a percentage of the GDP, the defence budget has seen a steady decline, reaching 1.74 percent of the GDP in 2014-15 and 1.55 percent in the BE of 2016-17. On the other hand, China spends 2.1 percent and Pakistan 2.36 percent of its GDP on defence. The budget presented to Parliament on February 28, 2016, set aside INR 2,49,909 crore for defence, which amounts to a 0.96 percent increase over the previous year's allocation. The budget has been presented with pensions as a part of the budget at INR 3,77,956 crore.

The capital budget has doubled from INR 37,461 crore in 2007-08 to INR 79,125 crore in 2013-14 and is approximately INR 78,587 crore in BE 2016-17 (Table 2.2. below).

Table 2.2: Capital Expenditure

Year	Actual
2007-08	37,462
2008-09	40,918
2009-10	51,112
2010-11	52,056
2011-12	67,902
2012-13	70,499
2013-14	79,125
2014-15	75,148
2015-16	77,704
2016-17	78,587

As can be seen from Table 2.3, the foreign exchange outgo is nearly 50 percent. In addition, in many of the major ToT produced items by the OFB and DPSUs, a high percentage of raw materials and spare parts assemblies and components is procured from abroad.

Table 2.3: Foreign Exchange (FE) Content in Capital Budget (INR Cr)

Year	INR Indigenous	FE (Import)	Total	% of FE in Total
2010-11	17,811	4,370	22,181	20
2011-12	11,905	15,258	27,164	56
2012-13	11,832	19,220	31,053	62
2013-14	15,990	20,927	36,917	57
2014-15	16,153	14,655	30,809	48

The expenditure in foreign exchange being large, the major plank in production policy is to achieve a level of 70 percent indigenisation by 2027. It has been estimated by the industry that the Indian defence market size is likely to be of the order of INR 86,350 crore by 2022 and INR 1,65,000 crore by 2027 on a conservative estimate. This offers a great opportunity for the Indian defence industry at different levels. It would also be the catalyst for a revolution in the Indian industry, bringing in technological upgradation, apart from giving a boost to the Indian economy.

Table 2.4: AoN Category-Wise Approvals (INR Cr)

Year	Buy (Indian)	**Buy & Make (Indian)**	**Make (Indian)**	**Buy & Make**	**Buy Global**	**Total Year-wise**
2010-11	60,863	16,710	15,845	19,450	40,547	1,53,388
2011-12	28,561	2,032	0	5,747	20,500	56,840
2012-13	18,689	385	1,004	13,460	27,114	60,652
2013-14	21,002	2,734	0	3,504	371	27,611
2014-15	38,319	72,751	0	0	6,760	1,17,830

Table 2.5: Outlay on Modernisation (INR Cr)

Modernisation (Capital Acquisition)	BE 14-15	RE 14-15	BE 14-15	Growth %	
				BE to BE	RE to BE
Army	20,935.41	16,927.35	22,054.50	5.35	30.26
Navy	21,911.99	17,075.24	23,360.90	6.61	36.81

Joint Staff	482.24	330.75	480.67	(-)0.33	45.33
Air Force	31,818.39	31,818.39	31,510.62	(-)0.97	(-)0.97
Total	75,148.03	66,151.73	77,406.49	3.01	17.01

Table 2.4 gives out the AoN cleared year-wise, however, there is a mismatch between the outlay for modernisation and the AoN, the modernisation funds being much less compared to the grant of AoN, which is shown as per Table 2.5 above.

Table 2.6: Projected Requirements for New Schemes and Committed Liabilities for the Three Services

	Committed Liabilities	**New Schemes**	**Total**
Army	20,513.44	5,665.48	26,178.92
Navy	22,248.12	4,091.00	26,339.12
Joint staff	328.04	561.14	889.18
Air Force	28,246.53	12,000.00	40,246.53
Total	**71,336.13**	**22,317.62**	**93,653.75**
Coast Guard	1,020.32	679.68	1,700.00

The projected requirements for new schemes and committed liabilities for the three Services are as per Table 2.6 above. Hence, the capital budget will be barely adequate for meeting the committed liabilities in the current FY. However, since the cash outgo for the new schemes may not be there for the entire amount in the current FY, the allocation may be adequate to meet the annual requirements.

Defence Acquisition Organisation: An integrated acquisition architecture was put in place in the MoD, headed by a Director General of Defence Acquisition. The Acquisition Wing has three main branches, one each for Land, Air and Maritime Systems. Each of these branches has three specialists, the Acquisition Manager, Technical Manager and Financial Manager, to progress all the capital procurement cases (refer Fig 2.2 below). Both the Acquisition Manager and Financial Manager are Joint Secretary level officers, whereas the Technical Manager is a Service officer of

Major General or equivalent rank. The idea of putting all three of them together is to ensure expeditious decisions on procurement issues, with adequate representation of all facets. A Defence Production Policy was enunciated in 2011, giving emphasis to indigenisation. Progressive amendments to the DPP since 2002 have enabled private sector participation and an increased focus on domestic production. There are perceptible differences from earlier DPPs. There is renewed emphasis on indigenisation: the 'Buy (Global)' decision can now be taken only after the other options for procurement, namely, 'Buy (Indian)', 'Buy and Make (Indian)', 'Make', 'Buy and Make with ToT' are ruled out; and by stopping the practice of nominating only the OFB or DPSUs as recipients of Maintenance Transfer of Technology (MTOT).

The defence acquisition organisation under the MoD comprises four key bodies which provide the basic structure for all procurement related activities. The planning process of procurement is under the overall guidance of the DAC. The organisation of the procurement is as given below.

Fig 2.2: Organisation of DAC

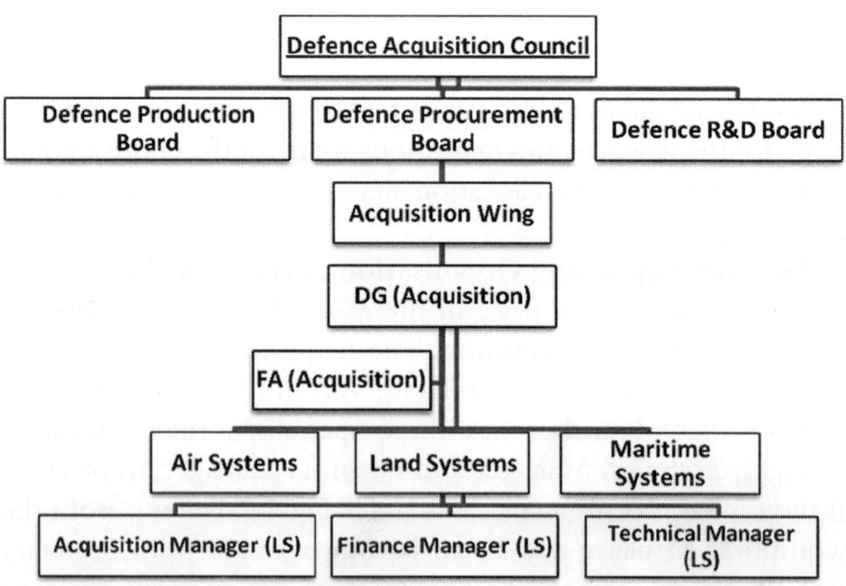

Defence Acquisition Council: As covered earlier, the DAC, headed by the RM, has the Raksha Rajya Mantri (RRM), Chiefs of all three Services, Defence Secretary, Secretary Defence Finance and Secretary Defence (R&D) as members. The DAC accords an 'in principle' approval for capital acquisitions in the LTIPP. It also gives an 'in principle' approval to each capital acquisition project in the forthcoming five-year SCAP. This approval involves categorisation of the procurement i.e. 'Buy', 'Buy and Make' or 'Make'. It also monitors the progress of major projects and the DAC decisions flow down for implementation to the Defence Production Board and Defence R&D Board. In addition, the DAC also sanctions procurements under the Fast Track Procedure (FTP).

Defence Procurement Board: The DPB is headed by the Defence Secretary and has Secretaries DD (P&S), Defence (R&D), Defence (Finance) besides the Vice Chiefs of the three Services. The DPB approves the AAP for the three Services and any amendments thereafter. It also confirms / modifies the *inter-se* priorities of the acquisition proposals of the Services and recommends modifications in the resource sharing for approval by the RM. It accords approval / recommends the scales of authorisation and usages of capital account items, and monitors the progress of major schemes. It sanctions procurement for acquisition from INR 150 to 300 crore and approves emergency purchases when necessary within the RM's delegated financial powers.

Defence Production Board: The Defence Production Board is headed by the Secretary (DP). It deals with matters pertaining to defence production, indigenisation of imported equipment and spares. It is also responsible for planning and control of the departmental production units of the OFB and DPSUs.

Defence R&D Board. The board is headed by the Secretary, Defence R&D, who is the SA to the RM. Its function is to advise the government on the scientific aspects of military equipment and logistics and the formulation or research, design and development plans for equipment required by the Services.

Defence Technology Council (DTC): The Defence Technology Council has been constituted under the chairmanship of the Raksha Mantri by the government to provide guidance and supervision of growth and promotion of research, development and production related to defence technologies. The DTC will assist the DAC in taking holistic decisions on specific defence projects related to long-term perspective plans and five-year plans.

Service Headquarters: The three Services Headquarters, viz., the Army Headquarters, the Naval Headquarters and the Air Headquarters function under the Chief of the Army Staff (COAS), the Chief of the Naval Staff (CNS) and the Chief of the Air Staff (CAS) respectively. They are assisted by their Principal Staff Officers (PSOs). The inter-Service organisations, under the Department of Defence are responsible for carrying out tasks related to the common needs of the three Services such as medical care, public relations and personnel management of civilian staff in the Defence Headquarters.

A number of committees dealing with defence related activities assist the RM. The COSC is a forum for the Service Chiefs to discuss matters having a bearing on the activities of the Services and also to advise the MoD. The position of Chairman of the COSC devolves on the longest serving Chief of Staff, and, consequently, rotates amongst the three Services. To facilitate the work of the COSC, a number of sub-committees have been established.

Finance Division of the MoD: The Finance Division in the MoD deals with all matters having financial implications. It is fully integrated with the MoD and performs an advisory role. To achieve greater efficiency in administration, expeditious disposal and transparency, the MoD exercises financial powers in consultation with the Finance Division as per the procedure laid down in the DPP and DPM. The DPP deals with capital acquisitions and the DPM deals with revenue procurements.

Stages in Acquisition Process: The procedure of procurement of equipment as enunciated in DPP, involves a number of complex stages. The detailed flow of the defence equipment procurement procedure is given in DPP. In a nutshell, the sequence of all capital procurement cases is as given below:

Fig 2.3: Sequence of Acquisition

Service Qualitative Requirements

↓

Acceptance of Necessity (AON)

↓

Solicitation of Offers (RFP)

↓

Evaluation by TEC

↓

Field Evaluation of Equipment (Trials)

↓

Staff Evaluation

↓

Technical Oversight Committee

↓

Conduct of CNC

↓

CCS Approval (if required)

↓

Contract / Supply Order

↓

Post Contractual Activities

Timelines for Procurement: DPP 2016 lays down timelines for completion of each stage of the procurement process. However, it has been the experience of those dealing with procurement cases that the laid down timelines are seldom adhered to a and generally it takes a much longer time for proposals to fructify.

Organisations Dealing with Procurement in the Army: The existing procurement structure for the Army consists of the Perspective Planning (PP) and Weapons and Equipment (WE) Directorates (Dtes) in the Army Headquarters. The activities, starting from planning to AoN, are carried out by the PP Dte, while after the AoN, the WE Dte takes over till post contract management which is the responsibility of the Master General of Ordnance (MGO) branch. The detailed organisation of the WE Dte has recently been structured to meet the requirements of the finacial powers of the VCOAS and enhanced to INR 150 crore. In addition, certain specialised functional-based cells have been established in SHQ which have improved the quality of GSQRs and RFPs.

Performance of the Acquisition System

As observed by the report of the Parliamentary Standing Committee on Defence on December 22, 2014,[11] the estimated losses accrued due to time and cost over-runs in naval acquisitions / developmental projects amounted to approximately INR 29,000 crore, an amount that exceeds India's healthcare budget for the year[12]. The committee has been severely critical of the poor state of equipment readiness of the Indian armed forces due to all major acquisition projects suffering from time and cost over-runs. Owing to "regular" delays, the indigenous aircraft carrier will now cost INR 19,341 crore from its original cost of INR 3,241 crore. Similarly, in the case of the stealth guided missile destroyer, the cost has been revised from INR 3,850 crore to INR 11,662 crore and timelines have been revised from 2010-11 to 2015-16. The report goes on to add in atypically strong terms that India's security has been compromised because of a fast eroding combat edge *vis-a-vis* its neighbours due to the depleting strength of fighter aircraft squadrons. The scathing observations spanning all three Services made in the report bear a rather uncomfortable resonance to the observations raised by the Parliamentary Standing Committee report of 2012, and if we go back by half a century, to the post 1962 War enquiry report which read as follows:

> Shortage of Equipment ; Statement by the Defence Minister Shri YB Chavan regarding NEFA Enquiry. 02 Sep 1963. "*The enquiry has confirmed that there is indeed an overall shortage of equipment both for training and during operations. The situation was made worse because of overall shortage of vehicles and that our fleet was too old. The enquiry has pin-pointed the need to make up deficiency in equipment particularly suited for mountain warfare and to make it available to the troops at the right place at the right time.*"[13].

The C&AG report on deficiency of ammunition[14] is equally scathing in its observations of the deficiency of the same with the Army. However, as per the information available in the public domain, the situation is said to have improved in the recent past. Certain important observations by the Parliamentary Standing Committee with regard to the state of readiness of defence equipment, in its report of December 2014, have been discussed in the succeeding paragraphs.

The report states that nearly 3.5 lakh jawans don't have access to bullet-proof jackets, It also states that the recommendation for purchasing 3,53,765 bullet-proof jackets were made to the MoD but the same have not been received. A recent procurement of 50,000 bullet-proof of jackets doesn't give any reason to cheer as it bypasses the DPP, with procurement through the revenue route[15]. There is also a shortage of artillery guns and missiles. In the case of ammunition, between 2009 and 2014, the Army had demanded

133 items of ammunition but the OFB managed to supply only 23 entities from the demanded list[16]. Ammunition of the 125mm gun, common to all T-72 tanks, was of bad quality and several times had caused barrel bursts, leading to serious injuries to the troops. The panel was surprised to note that the government was raising a mountain strike corps but no separate allocation had been made for it. "An amount of INR 5,000 crore has been earmarked for it but it is not over and above the actual budget allocated and the Army has been asked to raise this Corps out of its own budget,"[17]. The committee found that soldiers in high-altitude areas are short of nearly two lakh pairs of ankle leather boots; more than 13 lakh canvas boots are needed in the same areas, one lakh mosquito nets are wanted, and soldiers are waiting for 65,000 balaclavas or masks to keep their faces warm. The committee also voiced its concern over the fact that while the MoD seems satisfied that equipment like night vision goggles is plentiful, the Army has "an altogether different view." The report offers this indictment: "*It appears that the Ministry is not taking the Army into confidence while doing its perspective planning.*" There is a shortfall of over 40 per cent in the indigenous production and issue of T-90 battle main tanks that were to form the cutting edge of the Indian strike formations. Against a target of 300 tanks by 2010, only 167 tanks were handed over to the Army by 2013 by the Ordnance Factories. The committee states that the DRDO, tasked with developing technology for the military, has failed since 1982 to produce an acceptable INSAS rifle, the standard weapon of the Army. In the case of the IAF, India requires 45 fighter squadrons to counter a "two-front collusive threat," but the panel found that the IAF has only 25 active fighter units. "Moreover, 14 of these squadrons are equipped with the MiG-21 and 27 which will retire between 2015 and 2024, thus, reducing the strength to a mere 11 squadrons by 2024. The panel has observed with concern that our capability has already come down[18]". The panel noted that the Navy had inducted only one submarine during the last 15 years, while it had retired five. The panel stressed on the need to create adequate budgetary provisions to meet India's security challenges.

India's new aircraft carrier, the INS *Vikrant* (named after India's first carrier), has bust its budget by 600 per cent. It will now cost a whopping nearly INR 19,000 crore instead of the original estimate of about INR 3,000 crore. Additionally, three major indigenous warship programmes are collectively a whopping INR 29,000 crore over the budget[19]. The three destroyers of the Project 15 class, the first of which, the INS *Kolkata*, has just been commissioned, are about INR 8,000 crore over the budget. Similarly, corvettes of the Project 28 class, which are being constructed at Garden Reach in Kolkata, will cost about INR 8,000 crore instead of INR 3,000 crore. The Standing Committee Report points to glaring lapses in the pace of indigenous warship construction, particularly at a time when the Chinese Navy is growing at a very fast pace by inducting an entirely new generation of destroyers, corvettes and frigates. To match this, the Indian Navy needs to desperately induct new warships at a faster pace[20]. In 2012, the government's Defence Acquisition Committee had approved 198 ships and submarines for the Indian Navy. The present force level is 127 ships and 15 submarines.

While one can appreciate the problems in procurement of complex equipment involving absorption of niche technology , the deficiency of low-tech items such as high ankle leather boots; canvas shoes, mosquito nets and balaclavas cannot be justified[21] when we have a fairly robust acquisition structure in place. This can be substantiated from the fact that the Army has itself articulated its contentment about the decisiveness of the new government[22]. Also, there have been certain visible positive steps with regard to acquisition initiated on the ground such as the lifting of the ban from Denel ex South Africa[23] and an assurance by the MoD to promulgate a comprehensive policy on blacklisting of firms[24]. The DAC, in the past few months, has cleared a number of long pending proposals worth approximately INR 30,000 crore, taking the total proposals cleared by the new government since June 2014 to a staggering figure of INR 2,00,000 crore[25]. The latest step is the release of recommendations of the Dhirendra Singh Committee Report which has given extensive recommendations on the overall system of acquisitions rather than limiting itself to the DPP. The malaise obviously lies in India's defence capital acquisition structure which needs to be evolved further on the lines of the state-of-the-art modern programme management matrix organisational structures being followed by advanced Armies the world over.

A typical procurement case in the Indian SHQ and MoD in the present day and age is initiated on a 'noting sheet', with little application of technology. It is not subjected to a structured risk management exercise at the capability definition level which enables the government to take an informed decision about a capability sought to be inducted. At the acquisition level too, there is a zero application of best practices and enabling technologies as the Enterprise Resource Planning (ERP) for acquisition is yet not in place. This has resulted, to take just one example, in a shortfall ostensibly due to the glitches in ToT of 40 percent in the delivery of T-90 tanks by the Ordnance Factories (OFs) even four years after they were supposed to hand over the entire lot of 300 tanks to the Army[26]. Such situations are bound to precipitate given an acquisition ecosystem devoid of risk management, capability management and project management. The Dhirendra Singh Committee has recommended certain structural changes in the form of a proactive defence procurement executive, with specialist wings and personnel working outside the staff oriented environment of the confines of the government establishment in order to spearhead the procurement process, while, at the same time, working seamlessly with the MoD and SHQ.

Notes

1. Press Information Bureau, December 15, 2015, Prime Minister's Office. "PM Chairs Combined Commanders Conference on Board INS *Vikramaditya* at Sea", http://pib.nic.in/newsite/PrintRelease.aspx?relid=133265
2. "Review of Acquisition for the Secretary of State for Defence: An Independent Report by Bernard Gray" www.bipsolutions. com/docstore/ReviewAcquisition Grayreport.pdf. Accessed at 2100 hrs on September 18, 2015.

3. "India Ranks 76th in Global Corruption Index", NDTV, January 26, 2016, http://www.ndtv.com/india-news/india-ranks-76th-in-global-corruption-index-1270696
4. "Def Expo Attracts 490 Foreign Firms", TNN, *The Times of India,* March 24, 2016, http://timesofindia.indiatimes.com/india/DefExpo-attracts-490-foreign-firms/articleshow/51534120.cms
5. Rajat Pandit, "Global Arms Majors Keen on Modi's 'Make in India' Thrust, Head for Aero-India in Droves", TNN, *The Times of India,* February 9, 2015, 05.01AM IST.
6. Sidhartha, "RIL, Punj Lloyd Bag Defence Deals", TNN, *The Times of India* October 08, 2014, http://timesofindia.indiatimes.com/business/india-business/RIL-Punj-Lloyd-bag-defence-deals/articleshow/44659903.cms
7. "FDI Cap a Dampener for World Def Majors: 49% FDI Cap Bugs Global Def Majors", TNN, *The Times of India,* March 15, 2016, http:// times of india. indiatimes. com/business/india-business/FDI-cap-a-dampener-for-world-def-majors-49-FDI-cap-bugs-global-def-majors/articleshow/51403276. cms
8. "India and Russia to Jointly Manufacture Kamov 226 Helicopter Under 'Make In India'", http: // economic times. indiatimes.com/news/defence/ india-and-russia-to-jointly-manufacture-kamov-226-helicopter-under-make-in-india/ article show /50316231.cms
9. "British Firm Picks Mahindra to Make Howitzers for Army", *Tribune India,* February 18, 2016, http://www.tribuneindia.com/ news/ nation/ british-firm- picks- mahindra-to-make-howitzers-for-army/197898.html
10. Raghu Dayal, "Ease of Doing Business", *Hindustan Times,* March 17, 2016, http://www.hindustantimes.com/analysis/ease-of-doing-business-cut-through-the-red-tape/story-B93c3eDPEgKr9p182dlgMK.html
11. "National Security Being Compromised: Par Panel", *The Pioneer*, December 23, 2014, http://www.dailypioneer.com/nation/national- Security-being-compromised-par-panel.html
12. Vishnu Som, "As China Upgrades Navy, India Misses Deadlines and Busts Budgets", December 23, 2014 15:22 IST, http://www.ndtv.com/article/ india/
13. DR Mankekar, *The Guilty Men of 1962* (The Tulsi Shah Enterprises, 1968).
14. Pranav Kulkarni, "Indian Army Ammunition Won't Even Last 10 Days in Event of a War, Suggests CAG Reports", *Indian Express,* May 09, 2015, http:// indianexpress.com/article/india/india-others/3-years-on-armys-plan-to-fill-ammo-stock-yet-to-take-off-cag/

15. Rajat Pandit, "After a 10-yr Wait, Army to Get 50,000 New Bullet-Proof Vests; Needs 3.5 Lakh", *The Times of India*, March 31, 2016, http://timesofindia.indiatimes.com/After-10-yr-wait-jawans-to-get-bullet-proof-vests/articleshow/51624423.cms
16. Rajat Pandit, "Army's Ammunition Won't Last 20 Days of War", *The Times of India*, August 25, 2014, http://timesofindia.indiatimes.com/ india/Armys-ammunition-wont-last-20-days-of-war/articleshow/40862131.cms
17. Pranav Kulkarni, "Mountain Corps is Being Armed by Reserve Equipment", *Indian Express* , December 26, 2014, http:// indianexpress.com / article / india /india-others /mountain-corps-is-being-armed-by-reserve-equipment/
18. Rajat Pandit, "With Fleet on Last Legs, IAF Chief Sounds Alert over Delayed Fighter Projects", *The Times of India*, October 05, 2015, http://timesofindia.indiatimes.com/india/With-fleet-on-last-legs-IAF-chief-sounds-alert-over-delayed-fighter-projects/articleshow/44362873.cms
19. "Navy Pulled up for Delays, Cost Overruns in Projects", PTI, *The Pioneer*, December 24, 2014, http://www.dailypioneer.com/nation/navy-pulled-up-for-delays-cost-overruns-in-projects.html
20. Report of the Parliamentary Standing Committee on Defence, 2014-15, http://164.100.47.134/lsscommittee /Defence /16_Defence_5.pdf
21. Sudhir Ranjan Sen, Written by Suparna Singh, "Boots, Bullets, Rifles: All In Short Supply For Army", http://www.ndtv.com/article/india/. Updated: December 23, 2014 15:54 IST
22. N C Bipindra, "Army Happy With 'Quick' Government". *The Sunday Standard,* July 27, 2014 07:51:02 AM. http://www.newindianexpress.com/thesundaystandard.
23. Vivek Raghuvanshi, "India Lifts Ban on Denel", August 18, 2014 - 01:31PM , http://www.defencenews.com/article/20140818 /DEFREG03/308180006
24. Ajay Banerjee, "MoD to Change Policy on Blacklisting Foreign Firms", *Tribune News Service*, New Delhi, November 24, http://www.tribuneindia.com/2014/20141125/nation.htm#13.
25. "41Defence Buy Plans Got Nod Since June", *The Asian Age*, December 03, 2014, http://wwv.asianage.com/india.
26. Vijay Mohan, "T-90 Tank Induction Short by 40 Percent", *Tribune News Service*, Chandigarh, December 21, http://www.tribuneindia.com/news/nation/t-90-tank-induction-short-by-40/21041.html.

3. SYSTEMIC PROBLEMS IN THE ACQUISITION SYSTEM

The systems approach views a given domain from the paradigm of interaction between its sub-systems and components. The same has been discussed in detail in Chapter 4, however, to briefly explain what a system means, we can take the example of an automobile which can be considered to be a very basic system. Like all other systems, the automobile system too has a number of parts. Firstly, these parts impact each other's functioning through mutual interplay while they are of no consequence in a stand-alone mode. Secondly, the performance of one part affects the performance of the system as well of its other parts. However, the most significant characteristic of a system is that the behaviour or characteristic of a part will be entirely different from the characteristics of the system itself. Continuing with the example of the basic automobile system, we see that the purpose fulfilled by an automobile i.e. carrying of personnel or material from point A to B cannot be achieved by any of its parts individually. Hence, a "system", when seen through the systems thinking paradigm is all about interaction of its sub-parts rather than their individual action or excellence. Now if we apply the same analogy to the acquisition system, the purpose which the acquisition system as a whole is designed to fulfill i.e. meeting the aspirations of the defence forces through timely procurement of weapons and equipment within the allocated budget cannot be fulfilled individually by its components or sub-systems i.e. the planning component / sub-system, the budgetary component / sub-system, the procedural component / sub-system, the supply chain component/ sub-system and the structural component/ sub-system. In this chapter, we examine various components of the acquisition system in order to gauge their performance.

The Defence Planning Sub-System

The mandated process for higher defence planning for the armed forces is a complex iterative process involving a large number of agencies and is a major sub-system of the overall acquisition process. The National Security Strategy (NSS) articulated by the Cabinet Committee on Security (CCS) is the starting point for the process of formulation of the LTIPP. The NSS, however, is too broad based to identify or enable any real capability development. Hence, the vital document which would provide the basic guidelines for formulation of the LTIPP is the Strategic Defence Planning Guidance (SDPG) which articulates the contingencies that the armed forces may be called upon to respond in to a 15-year time horizon. The contingencies would be prioritised and fund availability duly earmarked for the same time span. The SDPG would be the key input for formulating the Defence Capability Strategy prepared by HQ IDS which would enumerate each type of capability required for each type of contingency laid down in the SDPG. Thereafter, it would establish the gap in these capabilities and prioritise bridging of such gaps. The next stage would be the Defence Capability Plan (DCP) prepared by the IDS which is the government plan for investment in equipment for development of future capabilities in the Indian armed forces. This plan too would have a horizon of 15 years and would list the capabilities required, with the associated timeframe, along with options for achieving those capabilities envisaged with the broad nature of each project and impact of each project on the budget. This, along with the funds, as indicated in the SDPG, would facilitate the formulation of a meaningful and achievable LTIPP. The DCP would be reviewed annually to cater to the changing strategic environment, improvement in technology and adjustments, if any, in priorities. The LTIPP would flow out of the DCP and would essentially list out programmes and projects required to be taken up to achieve the capabilities listed therein. The three Services would prepare their respective LTPPs which would be compiled by IDS under the Chief of Defence Staff after the force levels, force structures and force accretions have been studied and inter-Services priorities have been accorded. The LTIPP would be approved by the Defence Planning Council headed by the RM and, finally, by the CCS, with specific reference to force structures and equipment profile of the three Services. Acquisition will be affected based on the SCAP and AAP, which will flow out of the LTIPP.

All this is a very complex process and involves identifying the capability needs of the armed forces, establishing *inter se* priorities, examining options for meeting these capabilities, managing projects and programmes that flow out of the plan, and providing life-time support. The LTIPP contains a number of components e.g. *research and development and infrastructure development plan* and *equipment procurement plan*. Owing to the constraints of a developing economy and given the Indian strategic culture, the Indian armed forces, at present, are not carrying out the mandated higher defence planning based on the capability-based model described above and LTIPP formulation does not follow the mandated top-down process. The maintenance of '*forces in being*' or accretions is worked out on a stand-alone basis albeit through a consultative sequence at the SHQ and forms part of the five-year defence plans. An assessment at a tri-Service level is not carried out to ascertain whether *Capability A* is more desirable than *Capability B*[1]. Such analyses were, at one time, a mandate of the erstwhile Defence Planning Staff (DPS) before its merger with the IDS in the early 2000s. As has been brought out earlier, the planning dimension used to be handled by the erstwhile high level inter-Service DPS under the MoD created in 1986 to assist the COSC. Post its merger into the HQ IDS, this vital function has not received the attention it deserves. There is also no budgetary linkage between planning and budgeting at the planning stage which is a major lacuna due to which procurement schemes fall through at the procurement stage. Moreover, the perspective plans for the industry and the DRDO need to be in synchronisation with the LTIPP in order to achieve the timelines specified in the LTIPP for almost all categories of procurement. The plans of the industry, armed forces and DRDO need to satisfy an outcome that is desired by the strategic apex of the MoD, which could be the

DAC. This outcome would need to be in synchronised with the SDPG issued by a political body such as the CCS in order to be in synchronisation with the developments in other state security apparatus outside the MoD. The LTIPP, however, is approved only at the DAC level rather than the CCS level. Hence, the conclusion is that our higher defence planning is, indeed, flawed and impinges upon the procurement stage.

The Budgetary Sub-System

The defence budget is a subject which attracts extensive analysis every year. Usually, an alarmist view of capital acquisition is taken, especially in the last few years when there have been instances of transfer of funds from the capital to the revenue budget[2]. On detailed examination, however, it is revealed that the budgetary allocation in the capital head or the lack of it should not be a cause for concern to the Services, especially the Army, for the simple reason that the Army has not been able to utilise the modernisation budget allocated to it for the last six years in a row[3]. The Parliamentary Committee on Defence, in May 2015, had observed with alarm that the capital head invariably ends up in surrenders. The allocation *vis-a-vis* expenditure for the last five years for the Army's modernisation budget is as per Table 3.1 below. The under-utilisation for BE 2015-16 was INR 13,188 crore against an allocation of INR 21,940 crore.

Table 3.1: Modernisation Budget, Army; Allocation Vs Utilisation[4]

Year	Projection*	Allocation*	Utilisation
	INR (Crs)		
(1)	(2)	(3)	(4)
2010-11	19,177	15,641	15,856
2011-12	20,641	16,005	14,947
2012-13	18,971	15,749	14,760
2013-14	19,271	14,967	14,433
2014-15	23,832	21,933	14,843

(* note: all figures in columns 2&3 pertain to the RE stage)

Any major acquisition cannot be carried out in one year and a number of studies in the past have recommended that capital allocations and expenditure should be in the non-lapsable roll-on budget. This will enable the inventory to reach the desired figure of 30:40:30, as is the norm worldwide. The reason for under-spending the allocated capital budget is not a flawed planning process, as may be the popular perception. The concern about an impaired planning process stymieing acquisition and an apprehension that the LTIPP is not costed should not be there simply because most modern Armies in the present times follow higher defence planning under two contemporary approaches, namely, threat-based and capability-based rather than a budget-based planning approach[5]. The 15-year LTIPP, therefore, is a capability-building document in the true spirit rather than a financial one whose blanket financial approval covering the entire plan period or otherwise will have little impact on specific procurement cases.

What should cause concern to defence planners and stakeholders are the frequent instances of fully matured contracts failing due to procedural considerations, accruing millions of dollars in veiled expenditure[6]. Axing of the LUH deal after seven years of labour should be a major cause for concern. Similarly, the Medium Multi-Role Combat aircraft (MMRCA) deal too is being finalised after a long gestation period, that too outside the DPP through an IGA with France. As also, a 40 percent shortfall in the delivery of T-90 tanks by the OFB due to its inability to absorb technology for tanks[7] too should be a cause of concern within the nation's security establishment. Capping the Futuristic Infantry Combat Vehicle (FICV) developmental contract at the vendor selection stage and, finally, the impending failure of a matured contract for the Pilatus trainers should cause concern,[8] coming at a time when aircraft accidents attributed to poor pilot training are on the rise, devouring precious lives as well as thousands of crores of rupees in aircraft casualties.[9] Lastly, the committed liability greater than 85 percent[10] of the modernisation budget should also be a cause for concern.

The above instances of acquisitions going wrong have little to do with a depleted capital budgetary allocation, or approval of defence plans or for that matter a skewed capital to revenue ratio. It has everything to do with 'decision paralysis' and the inability to manage contractual risks by India's military and defence bureaucracy. The seven-year-old tender for the procurement of the LUH that was cancelled abruptly at a very advanced stage of acquisition on the basis of an alleged irregularity in trials, is currently under investigation[11]. The DAC, in November 2014, approved the acquisition of 384 LUH as 'Make in India' despite the urgency of the requirement and the accident record of the 'Made in India' Advanced Light Helicopter (ALH) Dhruv of which 20 aircraft were lost to air crashes in the last ten years. HAL too has fallen short of its commitment to deliver a prototype under the Utility Light Helicopter (ULH) programme sanctioned by the CCS in 2009. The MMRCA deal is in jeopardy amidst scathing observations of the Parliamentary Standing Committee on Defence[12] owing to, among other issues, the seemingly innocuous question of taking the ownership of 106 aircraft manufactured at HAL under transfer of technology from the French major Dassault. Though not seen as deal breakers, these issues have caused sufficient damage to delay the contract. The FICV project, which at a cost of INR 50,000 crore was lauded as India's biggest 'Make' project, was put on hold at an advanced stage in 2012 when the Defence Acquisition Wing under the MoD encountered an anomaly in one of the Expression of Interest (EoI) provisions dealing with the evaluation criteria of the successful developer. This event occurred two years from commencement of the contract, after the industry had invested crores of rupees into the project, thus, denting the credibility of the 'Make' process while simultaneously depriving the Services of this critical equipment [13]. Instances of a debilitated Technology Perspective Capability Roadmap (TPCR), and a rethink on the purchase of Avro aircraft by the MoD[14] after the private sector had sunk in millions to collaborate with foreign aircraft majors will inspire little confidence about the earnestness of the government's intent towards its private defence industry, more so with the government itself recently conceding that the 'Make in India' policy lacks clarity[15]. Discretionary cessation of matured contracts involving equipment desperately needed by the Services may appear to be a routine procedural matter on the face it. A closer analysis, however, would reveal symptoms of a deeper affliction in an acquisition system devoid of structures that facilitate decision-making.

Presently, the budgeting process is considered more as a mechanism for control of 'inputs'. The main emphasis is to account for, and contain, expenditure within the budgetary head allocation. Both the budgetary allocations as well as compiled accounts reflect the head-wise details for allocations made and the expenditure compiled, without any linkage with the details for the allocations made and the expenditure compiled, and with the specific purpose/ objective for which the allocation have been catered for, and the military establishment for which the expenditure is being incurred. Secondly, the prevalent system of budgeting and accounting is not conducive to effective and efficient expenditure control, which is the primary goal of budgeting. There is no mechanism by which the cost of operation of a mission as a whole can be ascertained. This is primarily because the present system of planning and budgeting does not require data either for planning or for preparation of the budget on the above lines, and, accordingly, the accounting system has not geared itself to generate such information. In the existing system, the annual budgets do not flow out of the long-term plans, except that limited efforts were made for the first time, in the Ninth Plan period to link the annual budget with the Five Year Plan projection. Since the Management Information System (MIS) that is generated at present has no built-in device which can depict the cost-effectiveness of the operation and maintenance of these facilities in the manner these are presently operated and maintained ,in the existing process , often, as in the case of capital acquisition systems, the resources get used on activities which are either peripheral or not critical to keep the military agile and equipped with state-of-the-art technology—indeed, there is no ready built mechanism to keep track of such expenses, to be able to eliminate the non-viable operations in the light of these deficiencies. While, on the one hand, no mean, full zero-based budget exercise can be undertaken, on the other, ad-hoc cuts or withholding of projects tend to do more harm in the long run, rather than bring effective reduction in the total cost of the project. The current modernisation budget of the Army for BE 2015-16 is INR 21,939.4 crore, with a committed liability of over 96 percent[16]. It now remains to be seen whether the MoD is able to spend this amount in the current fiscal. The present incremental-based budgeting system is, indeed, flawed and needs to be changed in favour of a programme-based budgeting system or the outcome-based budgeting system being followed by other government departments in India under an MoF directive.

Efficacy of DPP

In order to ensure that capability-building is carried out in step with the national security strategy, the introduction of the DPP for capital procurements in 2002 was an important step. The aim of the procedure was to ensure that no capability and, therefore, strategic, gaps, were created between the nation and its threats by ad-hoc procurement practices which had been followed up to that time. The DPP was in reaction to the prevailing difficulties in procurement, as perceived at that time, and has been in need for constant revision and upgrade. This is only to be expected, as the DPP was designed from early on to fix symptoms and not the root cause. The DPP (in particular the 'Buy', 'Buy and Make' categories, i.e. Chapter I) has, since then, been much maligned and bypassed whenever timely procurement has been necessary. Delays in procurement have since created such an unacceptable capability/strategic gap with our adversaries that there exists a perception that the DPP has prevented procurement. Being an evolving document, there is, therefore, a need to address the revision of the DPP ground up and not in a symptomatic manner if we want the document to become an enabler like similar ones have become in many advanced nations. The stated objective of the DPP is to:

> *ensure timely procurement of military equipment, systems, and platforms as required by the Armed Forces in terms of performance capabilities and quality standards, through optimum utilization of allocated budgetary resources; while enabling the same, DPP will provide for the highest degree of probity, public accountability, transparency, fair competition and a level playing field. In addition, self-reliance in defence equipment production and acquisition will be steadfastly pursued as a key aim of the DDP.*

If the stated objective, as given above, were to be weighed against the actual mechanics of procurement on the ground, it will emerge that the requirements of the armed forces are neither approved nor expeditiously procured. They are not approved in the true sense as the LTIPP does not flow from the NSS,[17] and the SDPG is issued by the political executive but is a compilation of the LTPPs of the three Services by the IDS and subsequently approved by the DAC. More importantly, no dedicated funds are committed to service the LTIPP in its entirety, given the extended time horizon, and the acquisition is not carried out strictly based on the LTIPP, though there may be differing perceptions on this aspect. Little wonder, then, that the modernisation budget over the past two years has been steadily declining in real terms, with committed liabilities between 85 to 96 percent while the approved priority list accepted in principle by the DAC runs into a few lakhs of crores. Furthermore, the timelines laid down in the DPP are rarely enforced nor is any one agency responsible for ensuring that these are met. The existing problems in the DPP stem from the statement of intention, the structure of its execution, the improvement in accountability and a need to refine the structure of the DPP.

DPP and Self-Reliance: The SDPG is a document derived from the National Military Strategy. This document provides the necessary guidance for creation of the LTIPP, the five-year SCAP and the two-year roll-on AAP. It is imperative that these plans achieve their procurement targets so that the overall capability outcome desired by the SDPG is achieved. There is no substitute to self-reliance in key military technologies which enable the unhindered growth of indigenous defence technology capability. The intention of offsets is to eventually gain self-reliance through reverse investments from foreign vendors. Foreign vendors are unlikely to part with key technologies without sustained negotiations from own side. The requirement of a roadmap to provide the necessary guidance to achieve technology capabilities is, therefore, implied through offsets in the DPP though it is not explicitly stated. Another aim of the offsets provision is to build the industrial capacity for self-reliance in defence production. The requirement, therefore, to achieve defence manufacturing self-reliance through planned capacity build-up is also implicit in the DPP.

Procedural Issues in DPP: The DPP provides operational guidelines for acquisition of defence products and services for the defence forces. Close to INR 95,000 crore have been allotted on capital expenses by the MoD in the current year, a figure that has seen more than 500 percent increase in the last seven years and is likely to see a possible 10 to 12 percent increase in subsequent budgets. The Indian defence acquisition process is fraught with unacceptable and undue delays at all stages and a substantial number of acquisition schemes result in foreclosure. Analysis of the cases of the three Services makes it evident that procedural propriety and integrity have overtaken the primary aim of effecting positive and timely procurement. Since the inception of a structured DPP in 2002, the number of acquisition schemes that has fructified has been limited. Even in these success stories, what can be credited to the procedure are repeat procurements which involve fewer stages than a fresh acquisition. Year after year, the success is measured in terms of cash outgo which does not represent the true picture of modernisation attained by the armed forces. The saving grace is that most of the high value procurements are effected through inter-governmental deals which reduce the unexpended portion of budgetary allotments for modernisation.

Every review of defence procurements by the Comptroller and Auditor General of India (C&AG) highlights deficiencies and omissions. Recurrence of mistakes due to sheer indifference and inefficiency can neither be justified nor condoned in the case of defence procurements where such mistakes can prove grave for national security. Analysis shows that unplanned procurements continue to prevent optimum utilisation of resources and perpetuate ad hocism. Delays continue to dog most cases with resultant cost escalations. Faulty parameters and inefficient trial regimes result in premature termination of a substantial number of cases. Flawed contracts lend themselves to multiple interpretations, failing in most cases, thus, increasing the hollowness. Subsequent disputes result in protracted wrangles and delays. Vendors raise the prices of spares arbitrarily, fail to provide promised after sales support and show reluctance to transfer contracted technology, and refuse to meet offset obligations.

Expenditure of enormous amounts allocated for the defence budget, thus, necessitates a critical analysis of the procurement procedure, an analysis of the delays, the causes of foreclosures and their attributability. Further, as repeated revisions have not aided in enhancing the effectiveness of the procurement procedure, analysis may safely conclude that it is now necessary to usher in revolutionary rather than evolutionary changes to the acquisition system. The analysis of the delays at various stages of the procurement process are as depicted in the graph below (Fig 3.1).

Fig 3.1: Acquisition Timelines Laid Down in DPP vs Actual (weeks)

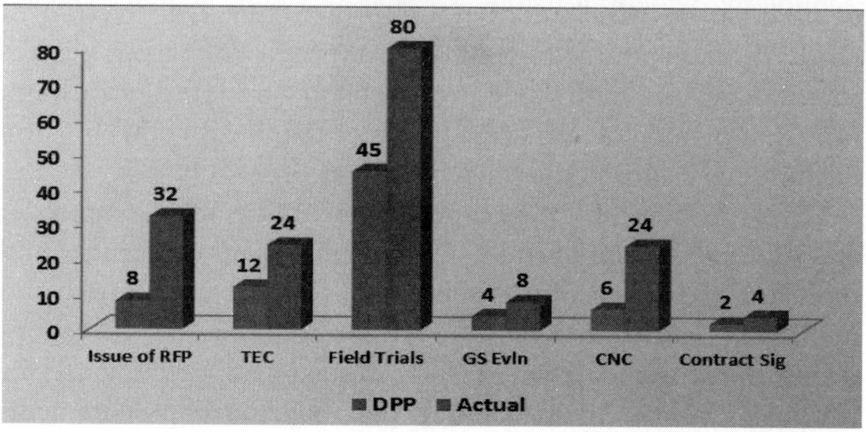

As brought out in Fig 3.1, the capital acquisition follows a sequential procurement system where the major stages range from the drawing up of SQRs by the Service HQ to the CNC and post contract management. These stages, more or less, practically cover the procedural dimensions of the DPP. There are some procedural infirmities in the DPP which have been discussed under the various stages in the subsequent paragraphs. This will help in reaching a conclusion on whether the DPP is a flawed procedure, and on the aspects which need improvement.

Services Qualitative Requirements: Formulation of SQRs is a complex process which not only requires analysis of the technology available globally but also needs visualisation of the futuristic technologies, keeping in view the procurement time. At present, formulation of SQRs which is a SHQ responsibility has been identified as one of the weakest links in the procurement process, causing foreclosure in a number of cases. Though there has been a substantial improvement lately in the preparation of GSQRs after the formulation of the GSQR Cell in the SHQ, the recent withdrawal of the RFP of the assault rifles does indicate that issues still remain and, thus, greater diligence needs to be applied in SQRs preparation. As per the provisions of DPP , the SQRs are required to be pitched at the basic levels at the same time are also required to be broad-based, realistic and of contemporary technology, widely available, so that it fosters a multi-vendor situation. An analysis of a number of cases of capital procurement from all three Services reveals that inadequately researched SQRs form the single largest reason, contributing to 70 percent of the failed schemes at the RFP and trial stages which ultimately leads to delays in acquisition. The issue is more dominant in the case of the Army because of the large number of schemes being handled by individual Line Directorates.

SQRs are evolved by the SHQ to define the minimum performance attributes, corresponding to the tasks to be performed by the desired weapon system / equipment. Thus, they have to be need-based, spelling out the users' requirements in terms of functional characteristics in a comprehensive, structured and concrete manner. Through the SQRs, vendors are told upfront as to what is being sought. Currently, all SQR parameters are classified as 'essential' and carry equal importance. Non-compliance of any of the SQR parameters renders the equipment unsuitable for procurement, as no deviations are allowed. In an earlier case of procurement of helicopters, the SHQ had laid down more than 200 essential parameters and every vendor had to be fully compliant with all, their *inter-se* criticality notwithstanding. A state-of-the-art weapon system / equipment surpassing all vital performance parameters can, therefore, get wrongly eliminated because of its non-compliance with some inconsequential parameter. Additionally, there is a tendency to spell out SQRs in imprecise, immeasurable and indeterminate language, leading to multiple interpretations and subsequent acrimony. In many cases, poorly evolved SQRs have resulted in non-fructification of major acquisition proposals. Once major flaws and infirmities come to notice, the RFP is usually retracted and the complete process reinitiated with the reformulated SQRs. Whereas for the defence Services and the nation, this means cost over-runs and delays, the foreign vendors find the whole exercise wasteful in terms of time and resources. A number of times, the operational parameters included in the SQRs do not conform to the operational requirements on the ground. For example, the span of a bridging system needs to be based on the actual obstacle profile of the adversary in the intended area of deployment and not on what is available in the technical literature of other countries. Even though posting of the RFI on the MoD website has been made mandatory for SQR formulation, the procedure still suffers from unsubstantiated information provided by the vendors. Vendors, in order to get their names included in the procurement process, generally agree to fulfill all the parameters required by the Services. There is no option with the SHQ but to accept the replies given by the vendors at this stage. Moreover, there is no provision to prevent a vendor from responding to the RFP, even if he has not responded to the RFI. The technical literature of a lot of equipment hides more facts than it reveals which tends to mislead the staff preparing the SQRs.

Staff dealing with the preparation of SQRs does not have adequate domain knowledge, experience and continuity in the job. The problem gets compounded due to inadequate manpower resources and professional pressures to produce results. Due to lack of application and experience of the dealing staff, the SQRs are poorly formulated and inadequately researched. Normally, the information available in limited technical journals and brochures provided by the vendors forms the basis of the SQRs. There is a dichotomy between keeping the SQRs broad-based and making them specific to avoid ambiguity at a later stage. Whereas broad-based SQRs are required to include as many vendors in the procurement process as possible, this sometimes leads to diverse responses from the vendors, resulting in problems at the RFP / trial stages; changes in operational necessity of equipment, resulting in revision of SQRs; unverifiable and immeasurable parameters included in the SQRs which result in failure at the trial stage; inclusion of futuristic and not yet available technology in the SQRs in the hope that this will be available in the near future is another reason for flawed SQRs. Even though there is an elaborate process of approval of SQRs through collegiate vetting at the GSEPSC and GSEPC, no realistic comments are offered by various agencies to improve upon the SQRs.

In order to prevent the issue of flawed SQRs, the Operational Directorates need to diligently scrutinise each parameter included in the SQR for its operational necessity. Standard formats for the issue of the RFI and for a response by the vendors should be formulated. There is also a need to carry out a more detailed interaction with the vendors in the form of the RFI for more accurate GSQRs. The RFI process has now been institutionalised in DPP 2016 which shall, therefore, enhance the quality of GSQRs in the times to come. All parameters in the SQRs should be measurable and verifiable during both field and technical trials by the DGQA and other agencies. The SQRs should specify the requirement of military ruggedised or Commercial Off The Shelf (COTS) equipment. GSQRs should lay down parameters in a definable range, specifying the lower and upper limits. This would obviate the issue of stringent parameters and also enable the parameters being verified in a realistic manner. The SQRs should be of contemporary technology and not too ambitious or futuristic in nature. Draft SQRs are circulated to a large number of agencies for comments, many of which do not offer any value addition. To obviate delays due to this aspect, the list of agencies to which draft SQRs are forwarded for comments needs to be pruned down after due analysis. GSQR formulation is a process which is open-ended and no timeline for the same has been laid down. Therefore, a strict timeline needs to be introduced to ensure timely receipt of comments from the concerned agencies. Elaborate professional interaction with the potential vendors at the RFI stage is crucial for correct formulation and eventual success of the acquisition process.

AoN and Categorisation: Although the LTIPP, SCAP and AAP give the roadmap for acquisition, as per the DPP, the start point of any acquisition process is the AoN and categorisation. AoN needs to be obtained for each case as it lays down the procurement plan and the budgetary support for the same. Capital acquisitions in the Army have faced little delays on account of the AoN. The categorisation part has, however, often been changed at a later date due to reasons ranging from a single vendor situation to the designated Production Agency (PA) falling short of expectations. Data obtained from Army HQ reveals that in a number of cases, the categorisation has had to be changed after a gap of almost two years. This results in the entire process being started afresh and loss of time, while the Services are deprived of the state-of-the-art equipment. Due care, thus, needs to be exercised during categorisation of equipment. Interactions at various Line Directorates, PP Directorate and WE Directorate on capital procurements reveal that the AoN is largely a sequential process and takes two to three months to complete. The delay is imposed due to the late receipt of comments and an absence of a collegiate mechanism to resolve issues in a collegiate manner which should ideally have private participation. There is also inadequate vetting of proposals before SCAP meetings and a lack of an integrated approach to categorisation by Acquisition Managers, Technical Managers and Financial Managers. DPP 2016 has reduced the validity of the AoN to six months from the existing one year.

Request for Proposal: The RFP is an all-important legal document and its correct preparation and timely issue is of paramount importance. It is a first step towards a timely acquisition procedure and any delay in its issue has a cascading effect on the overall timelines of the project. Presently, lack of a comprehensive database on cutting edge technologies, their vendors and realistic cost estimations are some of the crippling limitations for initiation of RFPs. After obtaining the AoN and financial clearance, the RFP is sent to the prospective vendors. Through this document, the vendors are requested to submit their technical as well as commercial proposals in a two-bid system. It lays down inviolable terms and conditions for procurement of the intended equipment including the entire range of activities such as technical evaluation, field trials, delivery schedules, payment terms, etc. The RFP forms the basis for formulation of the contract document governing the terms of procurement. Therefore, a great deal of importance is attached to this document as it is the foundation stone for the intended future procurement and it has a legal binding on all the concerned parties. An incomprehensive or ambiguous RFP, with incoherent provisions of the contract, can lead to serious issues, resulting in numerous technical, financial and legal hurdles. The successful implementation of any project is, therefore, highly dependent upon the soundness of the RFP. Moreover, the terms and conditions proposed in the RFP form part of the final contract. The complexities involved in procurement of weapon systems necessitate that the contract document is prepared comprehensively, which includes all issues relating to procurement, payment, post contract management, warranty related issues, legal provisions, etc. Thus, there is a requirement to prepare and vet contracts by a team of professionals consisting of users, and experts from the fields of finance, audit, maintenance, law, etc. A well drafted and thought out contract is a solution to numerous issues which may crop up during the execution of the contract. Presently, the task of contract formulation and its vetting is done by the same set of people who process the case. Generally, these personnel are neither trained nor qualified to undertake such detailed analysis from the legal, financial and other points of view. The vendors, on the other hand, have experts in the field employed to scrutinise the contracts and pick holes in them which are exploited by the vendors as and when required. The DPP, on its part, brings out timeframes for procurement of defence equipment; however, the document is silent on fixing accountability for any delay in processing the cases. It has been the usual refrain of vendors that the time assigned for the execution of the project in the RFP is usually inadequate. With a stringent clause in respect of delayed delivery of the contracted equipment incorporated in the contract, the sizeable Liquidated Damage (LD) pinches the vendors. On the one hand, the vendors are bound by a number of restrictions and the timeframe; however, no timeframe is attached to the Government of India towards decision-making, evaluation of the equipment and payment against delivery of the goods/services. This aspect has been commented upon adversely by a large number of vendors and the vendors have proposed the inclusion of Reverse Liquidated Damage (RLD) directed towards the Government of India, if it fails to fulfill its obligations as spelt out in the contract. However, due to obvious reasons, the RLD clause has not been accepted for inclusion in the DPP. It has been experienced that there is no formal mechanism of evaluating any contract. The difficulties faced, the errors committed or the lessons learnt are not analysed, and the necessary feedback loop has not been established to improve the system. No databank or lessons learnt centre has been established to learn from past mistakes/ best practices though the RFP Cell is partially filing these voids. Acquisition of defence equipment is a highly specialised field which requires experts to handle multi-crore rupees projects, with complete dedication and competence. Considering the complexity of the defence procurement system and the time taken in completing the procurement cycle, from conceptualisation to delivery and exploitation of the equipment, there is an urgent requirement to develop the required expertise and domain knowledge at the SHQ/MoD level. The dealing officers are inducted into a complex defence acquisition process without any formal training or experience, and have to learn on the job. By time the officer gains knowledge and just adequate expertise to handle his appointment, his tenure is over. This process not only results in knowledge drain but also, at times, helps the vendors to exploit the officers' ignorance. In the ever changing scenario in the defence procurement policies, the necessity to employ the best personnel for acquisition duties to obtain value for the money spent cannot be over-emphasised. The ills of inadequate formulation of contracts, leading to numerous problems during the execution and post sales periods have come to light in the case of a number of contracts studied. With increased spending on defence, with higher and higher allocations each year, there is an urgent need to train and induct experienced personnel for procurement related duties. Considering the importance of the issue, some of the leading nations employ professional negotiators, contract formulators, legal experts, the best of the user and maintenance staff personnel who have unmatched experience in the field to form part of elite acquisition teams to ensure value for the money spent. In this regard, the recommendation of the Dhirendra Singh Committee to create a specialised structure is most relevant.

The bottlenecks identified in the acquisition process, with specific reference to the RFPs leading to delays in procurement, can be attributed to frequent changes in the SQRs during preparation / after issue of the RFP. Also, the SQRs are either too specific or too broad-based, leading to no response or the resultant single vendor situation. The RFP procedure is a cumbersome/ lengthy one for all types of capital procurement, from a pin to a tank. There is also a non-availability of expertise for drafting a good RFP. There is also a lack of continuity and orientation of Service officers that affects the preparation of RFPs such as limited knowledge on commercial terms / aspects. The two-stage vetting of the RFP does not resolve all the issues. Since no mid-course corrections are procedurally possible or allowed, RFPs get retracted for every minor deviation though the latest DPP has sought to remedy the situation. The response of the vetting agencies is varied and they require more time for vetting draft RFPs. The various agencies for vetting are the Line Directorate, WE Directorate, Procurement Directorate, Ordnance Services (OS) Directorate, representatives for all three Services, wherever applicable, DGQA, FM (LS), TM (LS), JS& AM(LS). Hence, vetting by all concerned especially in the case of ToT takes time and causes delays in submission of bids. Repeated queries by vendors and requests for extension of time also cause delays in submission of bids. The issue of the RFP usually takes any time between three to nine months after the issue of the AoN due to the multiple clearances that have to be obtained; and budgetary support and vetting/ comments from all the concerned agencies. In case MToT/ ToT is involved, details comments/ inputs from PAs take considerable time.

Technical and Field Evaluation: The Technical Evolution Committee (TEC) carries out paper evaluation of proposals to shortlist vendors for field trials. There is a need to critically analyse the existing procedure of technical and field evaluation to achieve the desired results in a desirable timeframe. Many vendors forward standard product brochures with total disregard for the SQRs. The TEC cannot ignore these offers and has to read the small print to ascertain compliance or seek further clarifications, resulting in avoidable delays. Many vendors make false claims with the expectation that waivers may be granted subsequently, while forthright vendors may get rejected for non-compliance. Some vendors claim compliance only with the aim of having their equipment field evaluated in varying terrain and climatic conditions either for further development or for spicing up their brochures for the future. Vendors, especially from the Eastern European countries, sometimes misinterpret the RFP requirements or formulate unclear technical proposals primarily due to lack of knowledge of the English language, necessitating the TEC to seek clarifications. Very often, the clarifications submitted by the vendors in response to those sought by the TEC remain ambiguous, leading to repeated correspondence. Not all members of the TEC always possess the technical knowledge to scrutinise varying and newer technologies offered by different vendors. A study of acquisition procedures adopted by most other countries indicates that paper evaluation assumes significance when the technologies offered have to be evaluated either for adoption for further development of a system or when value is assigned to technologies to ascertain which equipment is technologically superior, to enable a buyer to make a more informed decision. In either situation, the task is assigned to technical experts. In our context, where SQRs of the equipment to be procured should be of contemporary technology widely available in the world market and where no value is assigned to technology while selecting equipment as long as it meets the SQR parameters, the objective of evaluation by the TEC, should be limited to ensuring that only the equipment that meets the technical requirements and serious players are invited for field evaluation, and ascertaining that the procurement process is not derailed when an L1 vendor becomes non-compliant to some other RFP parameters. Experience suggests that the requirement of "No Cost No Commitment" trials in the RFP, to a very large extent, also ensures that only serious vendors respond to the RFP. Hence, the objective of restricting technically non-compliant, non-serious vendors from being invited for field evaluation can largely be achieved even without examination of the technical parameters by the TEC. Thus, the objective of the TEC gets further limited to conforming compliance to the non-technical parameters of the RFP. Moreover, it can be argued that if paper evaluation was achieving its aim of ensuring that only equipment that meets the technical parameters is invited for field evaluation and if that conclusion was to be true then such equipment should, by and large, clear the field evaluation. However, experience does not suggest that. DPP 2016 has suggested a number of measures to improve the trial evaluation procedure, however, its efficacy shall be seen in the times to come.

The existing trial and evaluation process suffers from the following shortcomings:

Conception of Trial Plan: Absence of a well-considered trial plan is the primary reason for most of the infirmities of field trials. More time and effort need to be spent on evolving a scientific and methodical approach. All the parameters are filled in a standard format and sent to the trial units as a trial directive.

Issue of Trial Directive: Due diligence needs to be exercised in the issue of trial directives. Many aspects are imprecise and are interpreted differently by the trial units. A case in point is the field trial of vehicles wherein, trial units were asked to confirm whether the vehicles under trial provided adequate comfort to the driver. It is extremely difficult to determine and evaluate the 'driver's comfort' of competing vehicles, as it is an individual-specific and indeterminate quality. Such statements mean little and force trial teams to respond as per their understanding, thereby introducing an element of subjectivity.

Conduct of Field Trials: Field trials are conducted to obtain, verify, and provide data for the evaluation of performance and operational capability of systems, sub-systems and components to enable ascertainment of their mission accomplishment potential. As no Service equipment is ever used in isolation, its true potential can only be gauged when full-fledged exploitation trials are carried out in conjunction with associated systems. At times, full-fledged field exercises may be required to be undertaken to establish conclusive results. Therefore, the current system of nominating a trial unit to carry out validation of performance parameters serves a limited purpose. It neglects the suitability of equipment for integration in the existing equipment profile for mission accomplishment.

Life Cycle Maintenance Cost: The DPP stipulates that the concept of maintenance for all types of equipment should normally be based on an estimation of the cost of life cycle product support of the equipment. It further states that the validation of the support system and maintainability trials, integral to, and complementing, the trial programme of the weapon system should be held simultaneously, wherever feasible. However, the maintainability trials are limited to only ascertaining the degree of difficulty/ ease in maintaining equipment in field conditions. Maintainability of equipment and its maintenance costs over its entire life cycle are two totally different aspects and have to be considered concurrently.

Selection of Trial Units and Staff: Trial of new equipment with differing technologies is a highly specialised task. The trial teams have to be appropriately equipped and trained to evaluate equipment with diverse technologies and determine their *inter-se* merit. Additionally, they should have the necessary expertise and vision to be able to interpolate exploitation of equipment in a diverse combat milieu. In most of the foreign militaries, trials are performed by specially constituted 'trial groups', consisting of suitably trained officers having the requisite experience and flair. In India, trial units are selected because they happen to be located in areas where the trials are planned. Many trial units fail to comprehend the importance of trials and treat such duties as an added encumbrance. Most units are so overloaded with their own operational and training activities that they can barely do justice to the field trials.

Preparation of Trial Report: Trial reports often tend to be subjective based on the opinion of the chain of command and suffer from various other infirmities, which not only delay decision-making but even necessitate retrials. Final recommendations are not specific but couched in generalities where an equipment may be recommended for procurement albeit with provisos. Many trial officers feel that they are duty-bound to contribute their bit and, hence, introduce fresh parameters. At times, retrials have to be ordered only to validate these additional riders, howsoever insignificant they may be. In some cases, the field trial report is at variance with the DGQA evaluation report which is carried out concurrently to the field trials, creating a dichotomy in the process, and necessitating retrials.

Recommendations of Intermediate Commanders: Trial reports are routed to the SHQ through intermediate Formation Commanders. Many of them offer their comments without reference to the trial directive or the parameters against which the equipment is being tested. They fail to understand that they are required to confirm compliance of the SQR and not counsel additional parameters, their personal views notwithstanding. Formulation of parameters is outside their purview. Instead of a definite 'yes' or 'no', they qualify their statements with new and extraneous factors, leading to ambiguities and multiple interpretations. Introduction of new parameters at the trial stage and conditional recommendations tend to jeopardise the whole procurement case. In many cases, intermediate Commanders reject the equipment which has clearly passed the user trials on the basis of 'outdated' technology and want to include technology not yet available even to the advanced and developed countries as yet.

Objectivity in Evaluation: The shortcomings of the present trial procedure as listed above are linked in some way or the other to the lack of objective trial and staff evaluation. Due to the subjective procedures being followed at present, the final decision on the selection of equipment is made solely on the recommendations of the trial team and the Commanders in the chain. The shortcomings analysed pertaining specifically to the Army consist of unquantifiable or ambiguous parameters, and different interpretation of SQRs by trial teams. High quality equipment fielded by vendors at times fails in the trials for inconsequential parameter compliance, which impacts the procurement process adversely, e.g. not meeting weight parameters by a few grams. Sequential trials by the user, DGQA, and Maintainability Evaluation Trials (METs) and Electromagnetic Interference (EMI)/ Electromagnetic Capability (EMC) trials, like environmental tests, take an inordinately long time. DGQA lacks test facilities and depends on vendors to get the tests carried out as per its requirements. The MET, including formulation of the Engineering Support Package (ESP), is time consuming and leads to delay in submission of trial reports. Inadequate and dispersed test facilities and separate security clearances also cause delay in DGQA tests.

Commercial Negotiation Committee (CNC) and Post Contract Management: The CNC function in the DPP stresses on the need of arriving at the total cost of acquisitions. The components required to achieve the total cost of acquisitions consist of the direct acquisition cost, mandatory replacement of major components over equipment service life cost, scheduled and intermediate level servicing cost, and depot level overhaul and operating cost. The direct acquisition cost itself needs to be disaggregated into components such as the basic unit cost of the weapon system / equipment, accessories, ground handling and ground support equipment, spares package, Table of Tools and Equipment (TOTE), training and documentation, to enable analysis of the multiple dimensions of the cost build-up. Thus, the costing concept is based on the Life Cycle Cost (LCC) which is considered to be one of the more contemporary and realistic ways to determine the long-term cost of ownership. LCC analysis calculates the cost of a system or product over its entire life span in service and consists of acquisition cost and sustaining cost. It facilitates equipment selection based on total costs rather than the initial purchase price. It is also known as 'cradle-to-grave' or 'womb-to-tomb' analysis. A number of scientific tools and techniques are available to determine the fair price of equipment. To start with, detailed data has to be collected and collated to facilitate development of an appropriate methodology for cost estimation. Previous procurements of the same or similar equipment by any government department can provide valuable inputs as regards the cost-technology-inflation inter-relationship. Such a template, however, can, at best, be indicative in nature and would require incorporation of numerous other variables to generate meaningful approximations through analogy estimates, parametric estimating, software estimates, and so on. Development and application of cost analysis techniques and estimate interpretation require experience, flair and proficiency. Establishment of an acceptable price bracket needs expertise in holistic treatment of varied inter-related financial disciplines in acquisition that include earned value analysis; concepts and methodologies needed to develop operating and support cost estimates; total ownership cost reduction studies; 'optimal decision matrix' process and other management decision-making tools. In order to perform the above functions, the CNC must possess competence to analyse a contractor's cost proposal and evaluate his pricing justifications with respect to the established criteria. Additionally, an understanding of market forces, related commercial issues, cost/ price analysis techniques and the legal implications of the small print is absolutely essential.

The present CNC possesses little expertise in the above aspects as most members are 'generalists', with minimal domain expertise. The CNC is generally guided by the advice rendered by the Finance Manager who unfortunately, are perceived as unequipped towards providing any sound financial advice. A large number of this cadre possess a limited knowledge both of the military equipment under procurement as also of state of art cost estimating techniques with their domain competency being limited to accounting and audit functions rather than experts in defence economics. In a number of cases, if the benchmarking has been flawed, the price quoted by the vendor is at variance with the benchmarked price and, hence, the RFP is usually cancelled and re-issued, resulting in avoidable delay. The Life Cycle Cost (LCC) consists of deterministic cost (cost of acquisition/ development) and probabilistic cost (cost of operation, maintenance and failures). Whereas it is easy to calculate the deterministic cost, it requires a great deal of expertise to estimate the probabilistic cost which requires the necessary vision to forecast the long-term effect of local terrain/ climatic conditions, employment during operations, and quality of engineering support. The CNC is presently devoid of any such proficiency. Despite concerted efforts in this direction, LCC analysis has still not been adopted as an institutionalised methodology for defence acquisitions with a few exceptions. In the absence of any other alternative, last procurement price of previous contracts of similar systems with a standard inflation factor is used to calculate the benchmarking price which, needless to say, a rudimentary method. Inability to determine a realistic range of fair price hampers the CNC's ability to question the costing of the main equipment and support systems. Therefore, reduction in cost is sought by demanding discounts as a percentage of the quoted price, which is generally not a prudent method. Defence acquisitions also suffer from the issue of financial year syndrome. As per the present financial accounting system, budgetary allocations for any particular financial year have to be spent by March 31, every year, failing which the funds allocated get surrendered. In the first six months of the financial year, cases move very slowly and only start to pick up during the latter part of the financial year, peaking in the month of March. There is a need to ensure that cases are monitored for progress up to the General Staff Evaluation stage during the first six months and the latter six months are utilised for the commercial aspects.

Even if the contract is in the final stages of completion, non-completion of the deliveries by March 31 results in surrender of the balance funds and the case is required to be processed afresh for allocation of funds from the next financial year. This results in delay in execution of the project by a few months. The present system of financial accounting does not cater for such contingencies. Since procurement of defence equipment is based on the duly approved LTIPP and Services Acquisition Plan derived from the LTIPP, it is considered prudent to introduce a system of rolling budgetary allocations. This arrangement would facilitate timely procurement of equipment and, at the same time, prevent an expenditure overdrive in the month of March each year.

Negotiating Contracts: Advance planning and development of a well-thought out negotiation strategy as a part of an overall acquisition strategy are commonly acknowledged to be the key prerequisites for successful negotiations. Hard bargaining can be done only if own and vendor's strengths and weaknesses are known. Different vendors have different negotiating attributes. In single vendor cases, due cognisance must be taken of the vendor's known methodology while constituting the CNC. Many vendors submit inflated initial quotations to keep adequate allowance for subsequent reduction during negotiations. Special communication skills are required to gauge the vendor's approach and develop suitable responses as the negotiations progress. Contract negotiation is a highly specialised task and requires specific skills and extensive training. In addition to in-depth knowledge of the equipment, the negotiators must be familiar with different tools and tactics to conduct negotiations in a highly demanding world arms market. Negotiators must possess the necessary flair and be able to communicate effectively. Communication skills, both verbal and non-verbal, are a must for being a good negotiator as useful bargaining information can be extracted from non-verbal clues as well. Trans-national and trans-cultural negotiations require a thorough knowledge of the vendors' sensitivities and dissimilarities in negotiating practices. Bargaining is an essential component of all negotiations. Therefore, strong negotiating skills and optimum utilisation of available leverage are invaluable in striking favourable deals.

Constitution of CNC: Instead of tailoring the CNC to cater to the complexities of the specific system under procurement, it is constituted in a routine manner and the members are detailed to represent different departments without reference to their suitability. The thrust is towards ensuring that all the concerned departments are onboard rather than pooling talent. The DPP mandates a switch over to the LCC methodology of evaluating offers but the SHQ have yet to develop expertise in the same. As most members are unaware of the anticipated employment and exploitation of equipment, the application of LCC continues to be ad hoc and selective. The problem gets compounded where technology transfer is sought as an essential part of the package and has to be priced. The CNC has no financial experts well versed in international trade practices, foreign exchange transactions and contractual legalities. On the other hand, the vendors come particularly well prepared and accompanied by a battery of experts.

Lack of Data Base: As a certain degree of secrecy shrouds all arms deals in the world, there are no ready reckoners or well evolved guidelines for the costing of high-tech weapon systems. A well maintained databank can provide useful details of previously negotiated contracts of similar equipment to facilitate preparation of an acceptable price bracket. There is also a need to verify that there has been no downward trend in the world market since the previous purchase. Additionally, banked data provides clues to the behaviour and conduct of a vendor during the negotiation and implementation of previous contracts. Records of earlier negotiations also reveal the degree of flexibility displayed by the vendor during price fixation. It helps in devising own approach. It is equally important to maintain a database of the feedback of earlier contracts to identify weaknesses and gaps, if any. Although the DPP mandates that the Acquisition Wing should maintain the necessary databank, much more needs to be done in this regard. There is no free flow of information among the three Services. The Comptroller and Auditor General of India, in a recent report on capital acquisition, has pointed out instances when different

Services paid different prices for the same item from the same vendor. Another issue relates to quantification of spares required and their cost. In the absence of any supporting data, these are generally left to the vendor. In numerous instances, India has purchased disproportionate quantities of spares at enormous cost without carrying out any realistic estimate of their wastage rate.

Deficiencies in various stages of acquisition as flowing out from the DPP have been discussed in the preceding paragraphs. GSQRs and prolonged trials which are the domain of the Services and have been discussed in detail above, have often been identified as the main causes of delay of acquisition cases. If this judgment were to be taken at its face value, the FTP laid out in Chapter 4 of the DPP which precludes both the stage of laying down of GSQRs[18] and field trials should have been a resounding success. FTP, on the other hand, has been far from successful because since its inception in 2001, the Army and Air Force have been able to process only one case successfully through this procedure while the Navy has not fielded even one. Defence capital acquisition, therefore, comprises much more than only procedures, hence, the need for the DPP to graduate to a capability development document rather than being a contract operating manual, is imperative. This brings us to the moot question of whether High Value Defence Procurement (HVDP) is about procedures only or is there something more to it? Will revising the DPP every few years make the procurements efficient? What are the other factors which influence acquisitions apart from procedures. These aspects have been examined in the succeeding paragraphs.

Are High Value Defence Procurements Only About Procedures[19]?

HVDP systems are usually looked upon as something that could be made more efficient by merely improving policies, adding regulations, and refining procedures. However, this is in apparent conflict with the very approach of systems thinking. This is because of certain peculiar challenges specific to HVDP when perused through a defence economics perspective. These challenges pertain to the very nature of HVDP which is enormously affected by stakeholder incongruence, special market conditions, bounded rationality, asset specificity and various risks that can't be easily predicted or mitigated. Before examining these challenges, it would be prudent to understand the uniqueness of HVDP and its role in a national perspective like ours. Unlike the common refrain that lack of integrity is the prime cause of loss of public money in defence procurement, research has found that hierarchical control structures without accountability were, in fact, greater reasons for wastefulness (V. Rohila, 2011), supplemented by organisational behaviour. Defence markets worldwide follow a monopsony and purchases take place from relatively few manufacturers. Competition is weak even in the United States and almost absent in Europe, where national, bi-national or tri-national conglomerates virtually own their home markets;. The normal cost constraining behaviour of the free market is absent from military purchasing. Export regulations by seller countries and offset requirements by buyer countries further distort the market. As a result , the Military Industrial Complexes (MICs) of the superpowers have prospered over the years while the MICs of those receiving aid (like India) had no incentive to modernise their defence technology base. Post-Soviet Union's break up, the system slowly refined itself into a US-controlled monopoly. Whenever the buyers bought weapons, they subsidised the research and development costs of the manufacturing countries. The inability to price technology rendered them blind (a legacy of the post-World War doles that did not allow the Third World countries to develop their own defence technology). Gradually, this technology gap between the USA and other countries was covered to some degree by Israel and partially by the European Union. This rendered the arms market with the USA and the Russian Federation as major sellers, becoming an oligopolistic sellers' market. On the buyers' side too, various turns and twists in the world economy rendered the market becoming oligopolistic. The major buyers were China and

India. These market structures (everybody seems to buying UAVs from Israel or the USA) are still continuing. Technology barriers (like the Wassenaar Agreement) and niche product differentiation are so high that these products have almost become unique. It has now become an oligopolistic buyers' versus oligopolistic sellers' situation[20]. Again, market forces do not operate here. There is partial competition amongst the core technology sellers, but not enough to bring true market price competition.

Bounded Rationality: The concept of bounded rationality[21] propounds the idea that in decision-making, the rationality of individuals is limited by the information they have, the cognitive limitations of their minds and the finite amount of time they have to make a decision. It was proposed by Herbert A Simon. It would be, therefore, be imprudent to assume that buyers can execute perfect procurement transactions irrespective of the refinement in procedures. The behavioural characteristics of human resources involved in HVDP are affected by three major concerns:

- Bounded rationality agents[22] experience difficulties in formulating and solving complex problems and in processing intricate procurement information contained in the numerous clauses of contracts. A HVDP contract has sometimes as many as 60 clauses and sub-clauses contained in 600-800 pages of technical, administrative and financial intricacies, every single one of which has a direct bearing on the contract. These are usually not interpreted by Indians to their advantage.
- Opportunism as a trait is exercised by all the interest groups beginning from the government, at one end, to the seller, at the other. The government has a different set of rules for the public sector enterprises because as a buyer in public procurement, it considers itself the final arbiter. On the other hand, in a government-to-government contract, it may find itself incapable of exercising that opportunism. Often, there have been media reports[23] of concern about lack of spares support in the equipment bought via the foreign military sales[24] programme of the USA.

- Complex attributes related to lack of technological knowhow e.g. in India on composite structures (laminates), sensor technology, material technology related to cryogenic systems and real time spectral analysis, translate into an inability to evaluate the price of these. Thus, if one doesn't know the price of the equipment being bought, it leads to an obvious possibility of the seller exploiting this knowledge gap.

The result is the inability of the HVDP system to protect its interests in a perfect manner (O. E. Williamson, 1998). Transaction costs[25] go up. Given bounded rationality, therefore, it is impossible to deal with contractual complexity in all the relevant respects. As a consequence, incomplete contracting is the best that can be achieved. Cost estimation is a weakness across the board in the case of HVDP.

Life Cycle Costing and Defence Capability Accrual: There is inadequate data on life cycle ownership of systems even on equipment that is being used now for a long time. Perhaps there is also need for a cost benefit analysis (measure of effectiveness) that a particular procurement brings. For example, it may be a well worth exercise to compare the procurement cost of fighter aircraft to that of a UAV and assess the advantage that would accrue in terms of destructive power that either can deliver when compared on purely financial terms on a life cycle basis. An F-16 costing US$ 45 million can deliver 2 X 2,000 pound bombs in a single sortie compared to a Predator UAV costing US$ 25 million that can deliver 450 pounds of payload without any risk to the pilot. Would it then be worth it to buy UAVs rather than fighters? Ideally, life cycle costing comparison should be done for such cases prior to procurement. As long as these failings remain, the system will continue to err in costing estimates, causing overall loss of efficiency in procurements.

Asset Specificity and DRDO: Asset specificity is relevant as it ties up future trades to current transactions, when specifics about the trader become important in deciding who to trade with. Williamson[26] has written a great deal on the extent to which asset specificity should be organised. Asset specificity is defined as specific assets created to support the making of a particular equipment, for example, procuring a lens polishing machine to create sensor lenses for an anti-tank missile. Asset specificity can be said to include human and physical assets and even acquired knowledge. As more assets are created, the break-even costs go up. However, in the present era of complex and diverse technologies, high product differentiation can only be achieved in a small number of disciplines. The Heron (UAV) from Israel has a US-made computer whose central processing unit is produced in Singapore and on which codes have been written in Israel. If it was possible for Israel to produce that quality of computer at lower costs, it would do so. Singapore has sold US$ 350 million worth of 100 Bronco armoured personnel carriers to the UK, the erstwhile maker of the Churchill and Chieftain. The inferences from such weapon-making complexes and systems are clear. Low technology development with commercial civil use has to be left entirely to the private sector. State research and development enterprises have to move away from being the developer of too many to a more manageable number. Collaborative arrangements with nations and industries, like the DRDO has already done in the case of the Brahmos and Pinaka, are the order of the day. The present system of cost plus contracting within the DRDO has to move to a more efficient model. This may lower the research and development costs of our public sector enterprises procurement.

Stakeholders Incongruities: There is no one to blame as there is an obvious lack of a systems approach. Analysis of the interviews confirmed serious incongruence in the interest of the various procurement stakeholders. Perhaps the reasons are perceptional/ positional differences, lack of a singular systematic aim, self-perpetuating cycles and risk-averse structures. The interests of the various stakeholders can be interpreted in a wide variety of ways. With such diverse stakes impacting procurement, it is difficult to have a single aim of procurement and a complex picture emerges that is no way aligned towards the propounded aim. There is clear incongruity in the interest of various stakeholders. The political authority has to cater to a wide range of concerns such as electoral impact of unemployment, to seeing that the procurement systems do not falter and maintain a modicum of efficiency. The administrative bureaucracy is risk averse and the military bureaucracy has aligned its interests with the ethos of the administrative bureaucracy. The Line Directorates or the users often get exasperated at the repeated corrections they have to make and have little concern for the process. The actual end user is not interested in the process—only in the equipment itself. Also, these stakeholders have various sub-layers, with quite a few only concerned with system inertia, apart from being non-functional too. There is a strong case for removing such non-functional layers and making layers that add value such as a cost professionalising layer to the process.

Other Risks and Inefficiencies

Human Resource Weaknesses: A large turnover and lack of pre-appointment professional training continue to be the bane of the system. System rigidities prevent the MoD from fruitfully utilising the services of trained officers. The human resource function is a large weakness that has an impact as wide as poor qualitative requirement formulation to imperfect contract formulation to legal and cost evaluation inefficiencies.

Benchmarking Value Accrued: Capital equipment purchase can't be linked to a publicly available "National Defence Capability Index" which can tell whether a particular procurement has strengthened the defence capability by, say, one to two percent. Such a system needs to be evolved. There is need for benchmarking in other spheres like:

- **Service-Specific Capability Accrual:** For example, there should be clear benchmarking of the capability addition in the Air Force that procurement of an Su-30 squadron brings when compared to the Rafale.

- **Country-Specific Contract Performance:** How does procurement from the USA compare to procurement from, say, Russia or Israel?
- **Vendor-Specific Contract Performance:** Data on vendor performance should be readily available and accessible.
- **Life Cycle Performance of Major Weapon Systems:** Often the buyer is led astray by the initial cost of procurement. In case data on life cycle costs are available, such a scenario can be avoided.

Public Awareness and HVDP: There has been an increased awareness in the public at large about various major weapon procurements. The media has its own interest, which is selling the channel or the newspaper. Such news may even be based on unconfirmed reports or sources that may have their own interests. There have been instances of even the procurement process getting derailed. There have been repeated inquiries into the various so-called scams without much proof. The ministry is often at its wits ends when a C&AG report appears in public that appears to further highlight the inefficiencies. The public information apparatus, including service specific institutions, need to be able to argue scientifically and rationally on systemic issues concerning HVDP. This would address the concerns of the public at large. Because, after all, the government officials engaged in procurement are dealing with public money and, in a parliamentary democracy, the people have the right to know.

Ethics in Knowledge Management: The question of ethics corresponds not only to integrity in procurement but also associated processes like diligence in record keeping and handing over the acquired knowledge. Those entrusted with the moral responsibility of ensuring that knowledge gets passed from one generation of procurement officials to another, have not been able to do so.

Poor Risk Management: Even when contracts are signed, the risks are clear and evident. These risks are usually associated with the vendor attempting to integrate two technologies, integrate sub-systems, (for example, a weapon system to a vehicle) or the buyer is required to produce buyer furnished equipment. Contractual clauses like linking an effective date of contract to export licence clearance in the vendor's country offer a free window to the seller to delay his supplies to suit his interests. There is a need to integrate project management techniques and formal risk assessment of contracts prior to their implementation.

The Defence Acquisition Supply Chain

The supply chain can be defined as the integrated process of planning, sourcing, making and delivering a product, from raw material to the end customer, which ideally classifies the defence acquisition system as a fully functional supply chain. Going by the above definition, it is imperative that the supply chain drivers and flows should exist and be followed to achieve an optimal performance. The various drivers and flows have been shown in Fig 3.2 below and major cross-functional drivers of information and sourcing have been examined in greater detail in the subsequent paragraphs.

Fig 3.2 : MoD's Acquisition Supply Chain

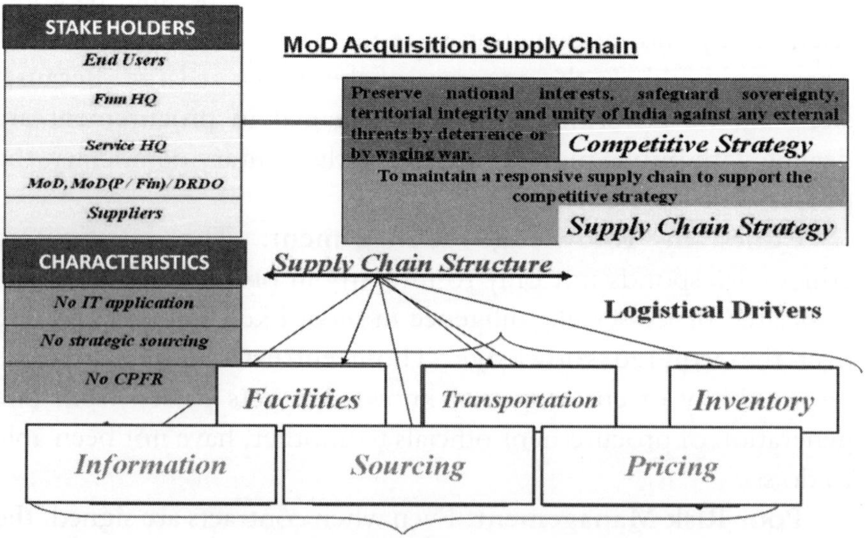

Contemporary Supply Chain Environment: Supply chain management involves the flows of material, information, and finance in a network consisting of customers, suppliers, manufacturers, and distributors. Material flow includes both the physical product flow from suppliers to customers through the chain and the reverse flow via product returns, servicing, recycling, and disposal. Information flow is the major flow that makes other flows function. Information flow involves all the steps leading to the generation of a supply order and post contract management. Information flow cuts across multiple functions and areas both within a company and across industries. Coordination and integration of the information flow within and across companies is critical to effective supply chain management. Such information flow is missing in the MoD's acquisition supply chain.

Managing these flows effectively is a daunting task as the supply chain of products or services for a multinational corporation can be very complex. The supply chain usually consists of multiple enterprises organised on the same lines as Army HQ, into various directorates. Furthermore, each of these enterprises is involved in a wide variety of supply chain activities such as domestic and international procurement, sustenance of the existing fleet, and servicing the post contract obligations. Owing to the structural and organisational complexity, communication between entities, and accurate and timely transfer of information can be extremely difficult. In particular, the multiple layers in a supply chain can distort the information flow. This distortion can lead to idle capacity, high manufacturing and transportation costs, faulty / delayed QRs, delayed RFPs, —and increasingly dissatisfied customers. Achieving supply chain efficiency requires accurate and timely information. The more complicated the chain, the greater the requirement.

In today's environment, the frontline forces or the end users are less forgiving of poor customer service and more demanding of customised products or services. As the competition and technology continues to introduce new offerings tailored to the requirement of the Army, suppliers have to respond by offering similar custom-made and highly personalised equipment. The ensuing proliferation of product variety for multiple countries, customer segments, and distribution outlets creates headaches in forecasting, inventory management, production planning, and after-sales service support. Finally, product life cycles are getting shorter. The expected life of a high technology product such as general purpose communication equipment is now 9 to 12 months. Additionally, technology is changing rapidly and products are rolling over constantly. As a result, the number of products offered by a company has increased significantly because product life cycles for successive products often overlap in time. The success of the product line, as well as the company, depends on effective management across the supply chain of both new product introduction and old product phase-out.

Supply Chain Macro (SCM) Processes: SCM can be divided into three macro processes or building blocks which are Customer Relations Management (CRM), Internal Supply Chain Management (ISCM) and Suppliers Relations Management (SRM). CRM focusses on downstream interactions between the enterprise and its customers, ISCM focusses on internal operations within the enterprise, and SRM focusses on upstream interactions between the enterprise and its suppliers. The fourth building block is the Transaction Management Foundation (TMF) or the basic Enterprise Resource Planning (ERP) system. TMF software is necessary for the other three processes to communicate with each other. The performance of an enterprise is closely linked to the performance of the supply chain. Successful supply chains, both within and outside India, have been focussing on ISCM for a long time and now need to focus on CRM and SRM outside the supply chain. The defence acquisition supply chain is still communicating manually with its stakeholders as the information flow in the form of real time, two-way information is missing. A good supply chain is not a zero sum game where the buyer can save costs at the expense of the supplier. It is a positive sum game where, if costs have to be cut, and supply chain surplus has to be generated, it has to be done by collaborative partnerships. Today, almost all areas of ERP growth exist within these three macro processes.

Supply Chain Best Practices: The above discourse brings out clearly that the acquisition chain is nowhere close to being an ideal one. The following best practices need to be followed by the defence acquisition supply chain to make it responsive to the needs of the users and become an ideal supply chain.

Best Practice #1. Use the Information Driver to Integrate the Supply Chain Partners: Information is a key supply chain driver as it facilitates the working of other supply chain drivers to work together with a view to create an integrated coordinated supply chain. Information is crucial to supply chain performance because it provides the foundation on which supply chain processes execute transactions and managers make decisions. To gather and analyse information, IT is an essential tool to facilitate information, whether it is in the form of a customised application or a COTS ERP. ERP has been commonly used for decades, in any mid-level Indian corporate enterprise, while advanced Armies have been using ERP solutions too for decades, having switched over from their customised software. This is conspicuously absent from the MoD acquisition supply chain despite the DPP specially enunciating setting up of an enterprise-wide ERP solution.

What constitutes supply chain integration? There are three key dimensions: information integration, coordination, organisational linkage. All three in the case of the Army supply chain need to be reworked. Information integration refers to the sharing of information and knowledge among partners of the supply chain. In the case of the MoD acquisition supply chain, the stakeholders in the supply chain would consist of all the agencies starting from the Line Directorate representing the users right up to the DAC and the suppliers. The buyers share information through a common ERP portal on the LTIPP / SCAP and AAP, while the suppliers share information on their capacity plans, production schedules and shipment schedules. The members also coordinate forecasting and replenishment. Is this being done in our case even with the OFB what to talk of private suppliers? The answer is no.

Coordination refers to the redeployment of decision rights, work, and resources to the best-positioned supply chain member. To illustrate: the Army that historically has developed its own upgradation for weapon systems may opt to give up its decision rights and let the supplier (at least the OFB or, say, TATAs, for its inventory) work out and execute the same on its behalf. The supplier may be in a better position to do the upgradation because of its superior knowledge of the product, the overall market, and forecasting techniques. This is the basis of programmes like VMI (Vendor Managed Inventory) and CRP (Continuous Replenishment Programme). Integration is not complete without tight organisational relationships between stakeholders. Executing a projectised / matrix organisation would automatically be taken care of through supply chain interventions. Supply chain partners need to define and maintain their channels of communication — whether those channels involve EDI (Electronic Data Interchange), internet exchange, or committees[27]. The roles, privileges and rights for the supply chain partners also need to be specified, integrated across the chain, and monitored. These systems have been implemented in foreign Armies decades ago. As per latest instructions of the MoF, e-procurement is to be implemented for all procurements worth over INR two lakh from April 01, 2016. This, coupled with the various e-concurrence models, shall certainly improve IT proliferation in the acquisition ecosystem. Just to take one example, from a scenario post e-concurrence: the initial draft of the GSQR formulated by the Line Directorate would be available to all the stakeholders in the acquisition supply chain viz the SHQ, DG Acquisition, MoD, MoD (Finance), MoD (Production) and DRDO on an open, all audience facing portal, accessible to the suppliers as well. This portal would already have the public versions of the LTIPP / SCAP / AAPs visible to the suppliers. All stakeholders will be given the time-slots to study the GSQRs and enter their comments once and for all. The comments of the stakeholders shall be recorded and a final GSQR prepared which shall be finally approved by the competent authority. A similar practice can be followed for the RFP as well.

Best Practice # 2: Develop an Enterprise-wide Technology Strategy that Supports Multiple Levels of Decision-Making to Obtain a Clear View of the Flow of Products, Services, and Information: To sustain reengineered business processes, many progressive companies have been replacing inflexible, poorly integrated systems with enterprise-wide systems or ERPs. The MoD acquisition supply chain too needs to do that. The MoD needs to build an information technology system that integrates capabilities of three essential kinds. At the functional level, the system must be able to handle day-to-day transactions and electronic commerce across the supply chain and, thus, help reduce lead times by sharing information on requirements for acquisitions. At the directional level, the system must facilitate planning and decision-making, supporting the demand and shipment planning and efficient resource allocation. At the strategic level, the system must enable strategic analysis by providing tools, such as an integrated network model that synthesises data for use in high-level "what-if" scenario planning to help managers evaluate plants, distribution centres, suppliers, and third-party service alternatives. Ironically, the information that most enterprises require most urgently to enhance supply chain management resides outside of their own systems, and few organisations, least of all the MoD, are adequately connected to obtain the necessary information. Electronic connectivity creates opportunities to change the supply chain fundamentally—from slashing transaction costs through electronic handling of orders, invoices, and payments to shrinking inventories through vendor-managed inventory programmes.

Best Practice # 3. Manage Sources of Supply Strategically to Reduce the Overall Costs: Determined to pay as low a price as possible for acquiring equipment, the MoD acquisition supply chain has not traditionally cultivated collaborative relationships with suppliers[28]. Defence acquisitions follow the principle of "the best approach to supply is to have as many players as possible fighting for their piece of the pie—that's when you get the best pricing". Good supply chain management requires a more enlightened mindset—recognising, as a more progressive manufacturer does: "Our supplier's costs are, in effect, our costs. If we force our supplier to provide 30 days of delivery period when 90 days are sufficient, the cost of that equipment will find its way back into the supplier's price to us since it increases his cost structure." While we place high demands on suppliers, we should also realise that partners must share the goal of reducing costs across the supply chain in order to lower prices in the marketplace and enhance margins. The logical extension of this thinking is gain-sharing arrangements to reward everyone who contributes to greater profitability. The government sector, however, is not yet ready for such progressive thinking because they lack the fundamental prerequisite—that is, sound knowhow of all their commodity costs, not only for direct materials but also for maintenance, repair, and operating supplies. This fact-based knowledge is the essential foundation for determining the best way of acquiring every kind of equipment and service the Army buys. With their marketplace position and industry structure the Service HQ can consider how to approach suppliers—soliciting short-term competitive bids, entering into long-term contracts and strategic supplier relationships, outsourcing, or integrating vertically. Excellent supply chain management calls for creativity and flexibility. For the first time, the Dhirendra Singh Committee Report, 2015, on revision of the DPP, made a distinction between military and civil procurement and talked of entering into strategic partnerships with suppliers.

Collaborative supply chain management integrates all suppliers real time to dramatically improve their performance. Integrating suppliers can help in minimising costs around new product introduction as well as ongoing equipment maintenance, upgradation and support, say, overhauling of the T-72 tanks. Involving key suppliers in product life cycles means higher performance and increased profits. Strategic sourcing enables enterprises to automate themselves through flexible mediums of portal and exchanges to drive down the total costs and reduce cycle times. Suppliers Relations Management (SRM) has provided a medium for strategic sourcing.

New technologies have made SRM a reality today. In the MoD's acquisition supply chain, the communication is still manual implying that the procurement process is sanctioned on file notings. SRM software enables sending and receiving information in specific formats which both the buyers and suppliers can understand. A catalogue management system enables aggregating catalogue item information from the suppliers' systems. The suppliers' portal solution is the online gateway for suppliers to collaborate on engineering changes, supply schedules, quotes, purchase orders, and invoices.

It is generally accepted that 80 percent of the cost of a purchased part is fixed during the design stage. Thus, it is crucial for a buyer to collaborate with the supplier at the design stage. Design collaboration can lower the overall costs, speed up the development time, and assist in system integration. Ford motors, for example, asked its suppliers not only to manufacture its components and sub-systems but also to be responsible for their design. To ensure effective communication, Ford required all its vendors to be on the same software platform for design. Ford also opened all its internal databases to its suppliers and co located its offices. Ford engineers were in constant touch with the suppliers and helped coordinate the overall design. The result was a significant improvement in cost, time and quality.

IT can be used extensively in sourcing in the areas of design collaboration by sharing of engineering, in the field of suppliers' selection, contract management and supplier evaluation on the several key criteria such as lead time, reliability, quality and price. Successful software helps analyse supplier performance and manage contracts. In the field of negotiations, successful software automates the RFP process and helps negotiate effective contracts. 'Buy' software executes actual procurement of equipment through creation, management and approval of purchase orders and post contract management.

A basic principle of good sourcing is that a buyer and supplier working together can generate more opportunities for savings than the two parties working independently. A long-term relationship encourages the supplier to expend greater effort on issues that are important to a particular buyer. This includes investment in communication and coordination between the two parties. This initiative, if not backed by the SCM best practices and ERP implementation, shall not succeed as desired. The issues of human intervention in an essentially manual system which inflict a severe time penalty to the acquisitions as also the problem of short tenures of the dealing officers can be easily be overcome by application of the information driver to the MoD's acquisition supply chain.

The acquisition supply chain is flawed to an extent that it suffers from lack of flows and drivers e.g. information flows, material flows , hierarchical interaction, as well as macro processes such as CRM, SRM and ISCM, essential for a standard supply chain. It is now time for the Service HQ to go in for the above interventions and put in place various interactions between components of the acquisition system.

Defence Capital Acquisition Executive Structure

It is well acknowledged by a number of reform committees as well as DPP 2016, that defence acquisition is a specialised subject that requires dedicated staff, apt in both quality and numbers, to obtain the stated success. The organisation must adopt the Western model of having an optimal mix of civilian and Service personnel specialised in various fields. Knowledge management has assumed tremendous importance in the present times. Most of the developed countries like the USA have taken acquisition as a serious subject and have special university level programmes / study on the defence procurement / acquisition subject. A similar option must be explored in the Indian scenario also, and the Indian National Defence University (INDU), when established, may take on this task at the appropriate level. To ensure competitive and fair development of the indigenous defence industry, a balance needs to be maintained between the DPSUs and the private sector. This can be ensured by having another Additional Secretary level officer in the Department of Defence Production to exclusively look after the interest of the private sector, especially in the wake of the government's recently announced 'Make in India' initiative.

The current procurement organisation headed by the DAC has only three specialist verticals, one each for production, procurement and R&D, each responsible for their specific outputs of a capability build-up plan. It does not have a programme vertical which would be responsible for the outcome of a capability build-up plan which is achieved within a specified schedule, cost and quality although this is a stated aim of the DPP. The existing acquisition structure badly needs a programme management vertical. The Dhirendra Singh Committee Report specifically brings out the need for an organisation on the lines of the ones in France, the UK and USA. The specialist acquisition organisations of France, the UK and US have been discussed in the succeeding paragraphs.

DGA, France: An organisation on the lines of the Direction Générale de l'armement (DGA) France has been recommended by a number of acquisition reform committees in the past. The DGA is the lynchpin of the French arms procurement system, mediating among the political authorities, the defence industry, and the military operators. After the Parliament votes the defence procurement budget, the DGA allocates funds among specific weapons programmes. Because of this power of allocation, the DGA can ensure multi-year funding of high-priority systems even within a shrinking defence budget. The DGA is a composite multi-skilled professional organisation and has, over the years, in line with the French government policy, been downsizing itself—the strength of the DGA personnel in 2011 was about 12,000, to be streamlined to 10,500 in 2014. About 85 percent of the staff comprises civilians, 5,600 (4,400 in 12 test centres, 28 technical trades) being technical experts.

Defence Equipment and Support (DE&S), United Kingdom: The UK Army carries out its procurement through the DE&S. On April 1, 2007, the Defence Procurement Agency (DPA) was merged with the Defence Logistics Organisation (DLO) to form a new organisation called the DE&S. The organisation defines itself as a "bespoke trading entity, an arm's length body of the UK MoD." It is headed by a Chief of Defence Material and is overseen by the Minister for Defence Equipment, Support and Technology. DE&S today employs approximately 16,000 people. DE&S acquires and supports equipment and services, including ships, aircraft, vehicles and weapons, information systems and satellite communications, as well as continuing to supply general requirements, food, clothing, medical and temporary accommodation. DE&S works closely with industry through partnering agreements and private finance initiatives in accordance with the Defence Industrial Strategy to seek and deliver effective solutions for defence.

USA: A major set of acquisition systems and procedures was established during the tenure of Secretary of Defence, Robert S. McNamara (1961-68) and during the tenure of Melvin Laird Secretary of Defence, during the first term of President Richard Nixon. The Blue Ribbon Defence Panel Report (1970) concluded that of the Department of Defence (DoD) established policies have "contributed to serious cost overruns, schedule slippages and [technical] performance deficiencies," and that reform would "require many interrelated changes in organisation and procedures." The panel concluded that the DoD could not fix the problems in existing management practices on an ad hoc basis, and recommended the Pentagon revise basic directives and create new ground rules to resolve these fundamental weaknesses. The report advocated the use of more civilian managers and the creation of a programme manager career path within the military, including industrial management training and experience, while giving programme managers greater and more clearly defined authority. It was recommended that Programme Executive Officers (PEOs) be appointed by the Service Acquisition Executives (SAEs). Each PEO would oversee a group of programme managers in charge of major acquisition programmes reporting up this civilian chain of command from the PEO to the Under Secretary of Defence for Acquisition. The Defence Logistics Agency (DLA) and DARPA have been associated with carrying out procurement for the US Army. A major step forward in the professionalisation of the DoD acquisition workforce was Public Law 101-510, which enacted the Defence Acquisition Workforce Improvement Act (DAWIA) in 1990. The Congress, considered the "three distinct elements within the DoD's Acquisition System: (1) the policies, procedures, and processes which govern the operation of the acquisition system; (2) the organisation of the resources (people, management structure, capital, and facilities) that execute the policies and procedures; and (3) the people within the organisation that make the system work". The directive states that the DoD shall maintain a proficient acquisition, technology, and logistics workforce that is flexible and highly skilled across a range of management, technical, and business disciplines. In addition, this directive requires that the Under Secretary of Defence for Acquisition, Technology, and Logistics [USD (AT&L)] shall establish education, training, and experienced standards for each acquisition position based on the level of complexity of the duties carried out in that position. The DoD has recognised the contributions of a competent workforce to defence acquisition effectiveness, in commenting on the cost, schedule, and performance shortfalls of defence weapon system programs. The DAWIA also provided for the establishment of a Defence Acquisition University (DAU) structure. Under the approval of the [USD (AT&L)], the DAU develops curricula for each acquisition career field, to include descriptions of the education, experience, and core training required to meet the standards for certification. These education, training, and experience requirements are based on the complexities of the acquisition job and serve as the basis for three levels of certification. Presently, the following workforce is involved in the acquisition related functions in the US.

Table 3.2: Distribution of Acquisition Workforce, US DoD[29]

Ser No	Career Field	Defence Agencies	Air Force	Army	Navy	Total
1	Auditing	42,31	0	0	0	4,231
2	Business	614	2,309	2,723	2,615	8,261
3	Contracting	7,165	7,996	9,125	6,041	30,327
4	Facilities Engineering	10	36	1,767	5,615	7,428
5	Industrial/Contract Property Management	317	26	75	65	483
	Information Technology	346	1,086	2,301	1,830	5,563
6	Life Cycle Logistics	230	2,762	8,962	5,415	17,369
7	Production. Quality and Manufacturing	4,838	406	2,004	2,353	9,601
8	Programme Management	1,230	5,361	3,491	5,601	15,683
9	Purchasing	251	131	358	536	1,276
10	Systems Planning, Research Development, and Engineering (SPRDE)	1,892	10,828	10,358	19,674	42,752
11	Test and Evaluation	317	2,936	2,298	3,022	8,573
12	Unknown	36	270	14	24	344
	Total	21,477	34,147	43,476	52,791	1,51,891

The Relevance of Structures: Indian Navy's WESEE Experience

The Indian Navy realised long before any other Service that defence acquisition suffers from a lack of structures, models and trained personnel to implement policies for successful induction of capital equipment. A small country like the Netherlands has 8,000 personnel for defence acquisition; the United States trains a plethora of specialists and has a Defence Acquisition University to train officials involved in capital acquisition.

Technology absorption is a multi-dimensional and multi-contextual subject which maps the entire life cycle of the equipment, system or technology used in the Services. The single visionary decision taken by the Navy which gave a fillip and started diverting the industry of ship-building to constructing warships was the setting up of a 'structure' in WESEE. The Navy devoted time and resources into raising a new cadre called Naval Constructors' Cadre and an in-house design house. The Navy realised that there is no one better than the user who knows what design he wants. The Navy provided the requisite exposure to its workforce in the Naval design field through a series of exposures and supplemented it with fresh recruitments in the design field. Results were there to see and the Godavari class ship was the first indigenous platform built in the country based on an indigenous design.

In the course of ship-building, the Navy experienced that weapons and sensors of diverse origin would need be assembled in the country. Russia, being a conventional source, was the principal supplier however recent engagements have fructified supplies from Western countries in addition to some indigenous products from Bharat Electronics Limited. Integration of these varied weapons and sensors received from multiple sources together was indeed a major task because DRDO at that time was a project oriented set-up and did not possess the skills for system integration. It needs to be well understood that DRDO always deals in technologies and not in system integration and platforms. A group of 20 naval officers and scientists worked together and a small organisation called WESSO was established to look into the Godavari class system integration. WESSO grew into the Weapons and Electronic System Engineering Establishment (WESEE) with its *raison d'être* is system integration. WESEE as a model came about to develop a technology base called system integration. Today, WESEE is designated as a system integration authority for the entire Indian Navy, and is at par with Multinational Corporations (MNCs) such as Lockheed Martin and Sylex that charge millions of dollars for this very job of system integration. This success came about not only due to policy formulation also with setting up of models and a structure which are the main ingredients of this success. WESEE today is staffed by around 50 naval officers with a minimum qualification of M Tech from the Indian Institute of Technology (IIT), 20 scientists from DRDO exclusively recruited by the Navy and assigned to WESEE and 300 odd software programmers and engineers from the industry as the corporate workforce. WESEE has been able to design a model system with intense domain knowledge in which the fundamentals of ship-building come from the Naval community, supplemented by the academia and professionals.

Right from the initial days of its journey, WESEE decided to follow the standards and processes of international repute, to preclude any chance of ad-hocism in progressing a project and is today producing combat operation management system for every platform of the Navy. The recently commissioned INS *Kolkota* and stealth warship INS *Kamrota* have a WESEE developed combat management system which was operationalised to 100 per cent efficiency from day one. System integration includes platform level integration; while the combat management system is an integration of information and data which is being generated by the platform. The complexity of the system can be judged by the fact that it is run by four million light support and 25 hardware nodes. This was possible because the Navy invested over a period of time in training manpower on the ecosystem for software development, backed by a foundation for running the software development life cycle. The Navy also realised that more elements and domains needed to be explored if it was to achieve a net-centric stature any time in the future. The next logical step was to integrate all the platforms together on the existing fleet, and data links was the solution for this. Link 11 is a famed US data linkage technology for the Navy and all NATO countries followed it up with Link 16 and Link 22. WESEE, in an early attempt, developed its own data link system which was conceived with the help of the academia, mainly the IITs. The fundamentals were positioned as foreign criteria, but thereafter, all the elements of the technology were brought together by WESEE. WESEE today is also a partner of a national project on software defined radio, a consortium of five organisations: two from DRDO, one each from WESEE, Centre for Development of Advanced Computing (CDAC), Trivandrum, and Bharat Electronics Limited.

A decade and half ago, when the Navy was going in for proliferation of IT systems in all the ships and on shore, it was realised that information security was going to be a new challenge. There was no thought given nationally in the direction of information security or no work was done in this field. As a part of the 'Wassenaar Arrangement on Export Controls for Conventional Arms and Dual-Use Goods and Technologies', a crypto system is considered at par with a nuclear weapon. The sanctions applicable to nuclear weapons and components in India are the same as those applicable to a crypto system, and WESEE decided to start working in this direction. The Navy approached all educational institutions of repute in the country but drew a blank as there were no scholars working on this subject. After a lot of effort, the Navy was able collaborate with the academia and today the entire cryptographic security of India's signalling system in the Navy rests on an algorithm called "Trinetra" developed jointly by WESEE and academia. Today, a catalyst sown by WESEE has grown into a full-fledged institute called the RC Bose Centre for Cryptography, Kolkata, and is conducting courses for all three Services and other intelligence security agencies in the country. WESEE is different from other organisations in that it did not strive to develop and generate a lab product for the end use of the Navy but concentrated on developing a product which is regarded with an absolute holistic view for the end use. In WESSE, the "user is the developer" and that makes it stand apart. There is a tremendous gap in respect to synergy between various elements involved in acquisition viz; academia, industry, policy-making, MoD and the defence Services. WESEE is a model that has succeeded and we need to invest money in such models and structures, as only policy-making such as in the DPP, will not help. It must be remembered that technology absorption is not induction; whereas practising technology is. Thus, there is a greater need to generate more centres that practice technology.

Systems View

Despite capital acquisition being a key focus area of the government, the Army has been able to conclude contracts amounting only to a meagre INR 6,000 crore in the current fiscal. To expect the new DPP 2016 to suddenly galvanise procurement may not be entirely justified. The refinements notwithstanding, the DPP remains a manual that essentially articulates the 'procurement process' that forms a relatively small component of the entire gamut of the capability establishment, comprising strategy formulation, capability definition, procurement, sustainment and discard. A cursory examination of the recent procurements by the three Services will exhibit that most of these bypass the DPP in favour of the IGA and FMS routes. The long undecided utility helicopter deal has recently been finalised through the IGA with Russia and an Indian private development partner, while the M777 howitzer deal similarly follows the FMS route. The DPP, on its part, in the last few years, has not been able to settle the Army's long standing operational hollowness in terms of Air Defence (AD) ordnance, critical ammunition, night vision capability and missiles purported to be fulfilled through over a hundred pending modernisation schemes, worth over INR two lakh crore, currently stuck at various stages of approvals between the Army HQ and MoD. As the acquisition community and industry fervently await the unveiling of DPP 2016, it should now be recognised, clearly and unambiguously, that the DPP as a capability building document has its limitations and we now need to look beyond it to address the acquisition structures. Structural reform of the acquisition architecture is the only way forward for achieving a transformational change in the acquisition ecosystem, considering that structures will eventually govern the organisational behaviour. To quote from the report of the Dhirendra Singh committee,

> A procurement organisation needs to have specialisation in diverse fields involving appreciation of technology, trial procedures, commercial negotiations and legal issues in contractual matters,

> estimation of costs, financing structures, and should also have project analysts and data scientists, etc. Since the focus would shift to production in India and indigenous R&D, specialists who have experience in managing industry and R&D projects, especially in cutting edge technologies with built-in uncertainty of time and costs, would need to become part of the procurement organisation. In addition, it requires flexibility in obtaining advice of consultants, and other professional bodies. This is best accomplished by organisations given a measure of autonomy and flexibility to devise their own procedures for activities, which would enable them to better perform their allocated functions under the DPP. Both the Departments of Atomic Energy and Space have benefited immensely from such dispensations. What is required is to strengthen the organisation by induction of experts in the fields referred to above and to give them tenures longer than now in vogue, and to many at support levels, full time careers within the organisation. The structure could either be an attached office or autonomous entity. However, to ensure seamless transactions between this organisation and the MoD, the DG(Acquisition) should have ex-officio secretariat status.[30]

It is, thus, imperative, that we address the structure of the acquisition system rather than just the DPP to achieve results. The details have been discussed in the subsequent chapter i.e. 'A Systems Approach to Defence Capital Acquisitions in India'.

Notes

1. Raja Menon, "A Mountain Strike Corps is Not the Only Option", *The Hindu*, July 29, 2013, 00:16 IST, http://www.thehindu.com /opinion/ lead/a-mountain-strike-corps-is-not-the-only-option/article4963979.ece
2. "Defence Forces see Rs 13,000 Crore Cut in Capital Outlay", *The Economic Times*, January 14, 2015, http://articles.economictimes.indiatimes.com/2015-01-14/news/58066358_1_defence-ministry-defence-forces-capital-account
3. Report of the Parliamentary Standing Committee on Defence, 15th Lok Sabha, December 2014.

4. Report of the Parliamentary Standing Committee on Defence , 16th Lok Sabha, April 2015.
5. *Approaches to Long-Term Defence Planning*, Strategic Management Vol. II, p.68, (Secunderabad: Department of Strategic Management, College of Defence Management).
6. Stephen P Cohen and Sunil Dasgupta, *Arming Without Aiming: India's Military Modernisation* (Penguin Books Limited, 2010), p.53.
7. Vijay Mohan, "T-90 Tank Induction Short by 40 Percent", *Tribune News Service*, http://www.tribuneindia.com/news/nation/t-90-tank-induction-short-by-40/21041.html.
8. Appu Esthose Suresh, "Defence Finance Wing Redflags UPA's Trainer Aircraft Deal", *Indian Express*, March 05, 2015, http://indianexpress. com /article /india/india-others/defence-finance-wing-redflags-upas-trainer-aircraft-deal/
9. "Armed Forces Lost 28 Aircraft, 14 Choppers in Crashes Since 2011", *The Times of India*, February 28, 2015, http://timesofindia.indiatimes.com/ india/ Armed-forces-lost-28-aircraft-14-choppers-in-crashes-since-2011/ articleshow/46403634.cms
10. Laxman K Behera, "Indian Defence Budget", *IDSA Comment*, March 04, 2013. http://www.idsa.in/idsacomments/ IndiasDefenceBudget2013-14_ lkbehera_040313
11. "Government Scraps Rs. 6,000-cr Tender for Light Utility Helicopters", PTI, *The Hindu Business Line*, August 29, 2014, https:// www. google. co.in/ webhp?sourceid = chrome-instant&rlz=1C1AVSX_ enIN409&ion=1&espv=2&ie=UTF-8#q=helicopter+deal+cancelled+ second+time+in+7+years.
12. "National Security Being Compromised: Par Panel", *The Pioneer*, December 23, 2014, http://www.dailypioneer.com/nation/national-security-being-compromised-par-panel.html - See more at: http://www.claws.in/1321/ mismanage-projects-and-lose-money-vikram-Taneja.html# sthash .4xc87fXg.dpuf
13. Ajai Shukla, "Setback for Private Defence Industry", *Business Standard* (New Delhi), October 22, 2012, http://www.business-standard.com/article/ economy-policy/setback-for-private-defence-industry-112102202022_1.html
14. Ajai Shukla, "Def Min Questions the Need to Replace Avro", *Business Standard*, December 18, 2014, http://www.business-standard.com/article/economy-policy/defmin-questions-the-need-to-replace-avro-114121800066_1.html.
15. Chethan Kumar, "Make in India Lacks Clarity", *The Times of India*, February 19, 2015, http://timesofindia.indiatimes.com/india/Make-in-India-plan-lacks-clarity-admits-Manohar-Parrikar/articleshow/46293546.cms

16. Laxman K Behera, "India's Defence Budget 2015-16", *IDSA Issue Brief*, March 02, 2016, http:// www. idsa.in / issue brief/IndiasDefenceBudget2015-16_lkbehera_020315
17. India does not have an articulated National Security Strategy.The apex planning document from which the long-term defence planning is carried out by the Services is the 'Raksha Mantri's Operational Directive' issued every five years. The last such Operational Directive was issued in 2010.
18. The Fast Track Procedure for meeting urgent operational requirements was promulgated vide MoD ID No: 800/SS (A)/2001 dated September 28, 2001. There is no requirement of General Staff Qualitative Requirements through the Service Equipment Policy Committee, however, Operational Requirements need to be drawn for carrying out procurement under this procedure.
19. Vikas Rohilla, "Are High Value Defence Procurements Only About Procedures?" *Defence Management Journal,* College of Defence Management, September 2011.
20. As per SIPRI estimates of 2014.
21. Herbert Simon was a 1978 Nobel Prize winner in economics whose research ranged across fields of cognitive psychology, public administration and economics. He coined the term "bounded rationality".
22. Oliver E Williamson, 2009, Nobel Prize winner in economics, has talked about the difficulties of individuals to process information when they deal with complex subjects.
23. "Transparency versus Urgency of Acquisition", September 12, 2010, Securityrisks.com http://www.security-risks.com/security-issues-south-asia/missiles/defence-procurement-transparency-versus-urgency-of-acquisitions-819.html
24. The Foreign Military Sales Programme is a US government to other governments system of sales of defence equipment.
25. Transactions are the basis of economic thinking and the term transaction cost has been coined by Ronald Coase, a 1991 Nobel Laureate in economics. A transaction cost is said to be a cost associated with, say, a commission paid to a broker in buying or selling a stock, investment of physical or mental energy or risk associated with a transaction.
26. n.22.
27. Defence acquisitions are being carried out through a number of committees which carry out collegiate vetting of the proposals viz the lower committee or the SCAPCC, the higher committee or the SCAPCHC, the Defence Procurement Board and the Defence Acquisition Council.

28. "Committee of Experts for Amendment to DPP-2013 Including Formulation of Policy Framework", http://www.mod.nic.in/ writer ead data/ Reportddp.pdf. Accessed on 2100 hrs on September, 2015. Para 3.3.03 talks of a strategic partnership with private sector.
29. Ibid., "Dedicated Acquisition Organisations & Training of Acquisition Work Force". Para 6.6.06, Annexure 2.
30. Ibid., para 6.6.04.

4. A SYSTEMS APPROACH TO DEFENCE CAPITAL ACQUISITIONS IN INDIA

Systems Approach and its Relevance to Defence Acquisitions

It needs no elaboration that the scope of high value defence procurements spans much beyond the mere procedural dimension.[1] The organisational structure, which has a major role to play in defence capital acquisition,[2] has remained largely unchanged since the setting up of the Director General of Acquisition in the Ministry of Defence (MoD) on the recommendations of the Group of Ministers (GoM) Report post Kargil conflict. Organisational structure is accorded a very high degree of importance in 'systems thinking' and this chapter examines the acquisition structure reform options generated through the systems approach as applicable currently to the Indian scenario. Post 1930s, three different models of management, the traditional approach, human relations theory and systems theory, competed for precedence. The traditional approach was based on Taylor's scientific theory, Fayol's administrative management theory and Weber's bureaucracy theory. It was in the 1960s that, because of the weaknesses of the traditional and human relationships models, and its own inherent superiority, that the systems approach came to dominate the management landscape. George Wilhelm Hegel (1770-1831) was the German philosopher who is credited as being a pioneer in 'systems' thinking and had propounded the following postulates:

- **The whole is more than the sum of parts.** The system as a whole has an objective which may not be explained by the sum of the parts. The study of the parts alone will not explain the whole system.
- **The whole determines the nature of the parts**. The same part may perform different roles in different systems.

- **The parts cannot be understood if considered in isolation from the whole**. The role played by the part is determined by the whole.
- **The parts are dynamically inter-related and inter-dependent.** For understanding a system, it is important to understand and analyse such inter-relationships.

The systems approach examines a discipline from the paradigm of interaction between its components rather than focussing on their individual behaviour. One of the most significant characteristics of a system, as brought out above, is that the behaviour of a part or a component or a sub-system will be entirely different from the behaviour of the system as a whole. If this analogy is applied to the acquisition system, the purpose which the acquisition system as a whole is designed to fulfill i.e. *meeting the aspirations of the defence forces through timely procurement of weapons and equipment within the allocated budget*, cannot be achieved individually by its components or sub-systems i.e. the planning sub-system, the budgetary sub-system, the procedural sub-system, the supply chain sub-system and the structural sub-system—it can be fulfilled only through an ideal interaction of all these sub-systems.

Cause and Effect Relationship in Acquisitions: Causal loops are often used in the systems approach to solve complex problems under the systems dynamics approach. Eleven laws of systems theory propounded by Peter Senge[3] are applicable to all complex issues, including the acquisition system. The connectedness / inter-relationship between the various components of a system is fundamental to systems thinking. This connectedness is expressed by the Causal Loop Diagram (CLD) which is a visual depiction of a complex system. The causal loops typically evolve into system archetypes which depict a distinctive combination of reinforcing and balancing loops. One of the afflictions of 'procurement scams' that plague the acquisition system in India has been expressed through a CLD and explained below through the system archetype, 'Fixes that Fail'.

Fig 4.1: Acquisition Causal Loop

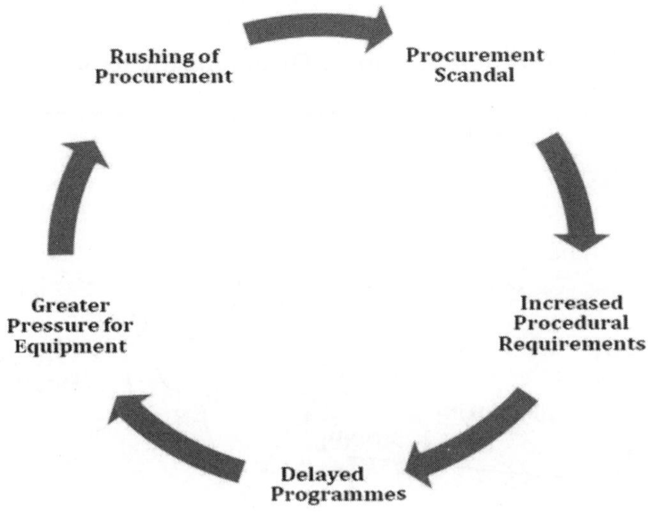

FIXES THAT FAIL

Acquisition programmes in India are usually delayed due to various reasons. The greater this delay, the greater the pressure on the acquisition system to procure equipment faster. The greater the pressure to procure, the greater the hurry, and the acquisition system rushes for procurement. The greater the rush, the greater the chances of a procurement scam. The more the chances of a procurement scam, the greater are the short-term checks and balances introduced by the government in terms of probity and accountability, resulting in delayed programmes again. Hence, if we apply short-term "**fixes**" instead of actual, long-term reforms, they are bound to be counter-productive.

The acquisition system, therefore, is not a process but is actually a "system" conforming to the tenets of the systems theory. A system is defined as "*an identifiable, complex and dynamic element having an objective and is composed of discernible different elements or sub-systems that are inter-related to, and inter-dependent on, each other; and the whole element has an overall capability to maintain stability and to adapt to behavior in respect to external influence*".

The acquisition system can, thus, be represented with the help of a diagram as under:

Fig 4.2: Acquisition System: A Diagrammatic Representation

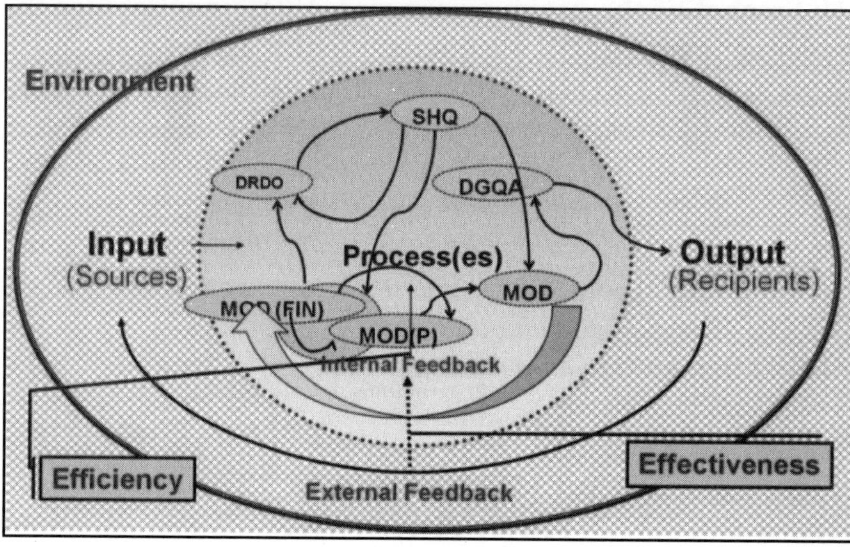

The acquisition organisation meets all the prerequisites of a system, i.e. it has well defined objectives, and consists of sub-systems/elements in the form of departments. These sub-systems are inter-related and inter-dependent. Any change in the elements or their relationships will result in a change in the system or its organisation as a whole. There is a flow of regular information in the organisation which takes feedback from the relevant departments and undergoes constant changes to achieve the goals and objectives. The components of the acquisition system comprise the SHQ, the MoD, the MoD (Production), the MoD (Finance), DRDO, DGQA, etc, as together they make the acquisition system work. There is a definitive system boundary and the corporate sector dealing with acquisition, end users as well as the other government departments such as the Department of Industrial Policy and Promotion (DIPP), etc which control the policies affecting acquisition, lie outside this boundary. Every system has a system ownership and these system owners are likely to be senior managers who can cause the system to change significantly or cease to exist. Stake-holding employees of the organisation or individuals with an operational role in the system, namely, the SHQ cannot be the system owners since they cannot change the system significantly. In the acquisition system, the system owners are the MoD, MoD (Production) and MoD(Finance) that wield the authority to control the system.

A process such as the DPP is a transformation or a series of transformations brought about in the throughput of a system as a result of which the same transforms in shape, size, and version. Processes differ from structures in the sense that they consist of states rather than elements and relations. A process is more dynamic in nature and gets easily influenced by the internal and external environments and the changes in the process, thus, are frequent. A structure, on the other hand, refers to a set of relations that has a positional value and is relatively stable in nature, having lasting components which either carry out processes or are acted upon by the processes. In keeping with the universal trend, the acquisition organisation too is structure-based wherein the presence of human beings fosters a resistance to change. The mismatch between structures and processes is responsible for a large number of systemic problems. Given the above dynamics, revising only the procedural aspects of the DPP year after year may result in only marginal improvement in the overall acquisition ecosystem. The performance of the acquisition system has not shown any dramatic improvement despite successive versions of the DPP because it is not being treated as a complex, multi-layered non-linear system which it actually is, and needs to be viewed as a whole which is much more than the sum of its parts.[4] The entire effort of the policy-makers is concentrated towards refining only the processes while the archaic organisational structure responsible for their execution remains unaddressed. Systems thinking professes that organisations usually react to events visible to them and make immediate changes to the processes so that those events do not recur. Reacting to events only brings about a transitory change. As per the tenets of systems thinking (Fig 4.3 below), the patterns and trends which emerge from the series of events need to be recognised and changes implemented accordingly, which again, will not be of a permanent nature. If a permanent change is desired, the structures on which these processes ride, need to be addressed. Going beyond change, if the stakeholder seeks a transformation, mathematical models intended to capture the fundamental interactions between the system and its environment will need to be put in place and later validated to measure its performance[5].

Fig 4.3: Tenets of Systems Thinking

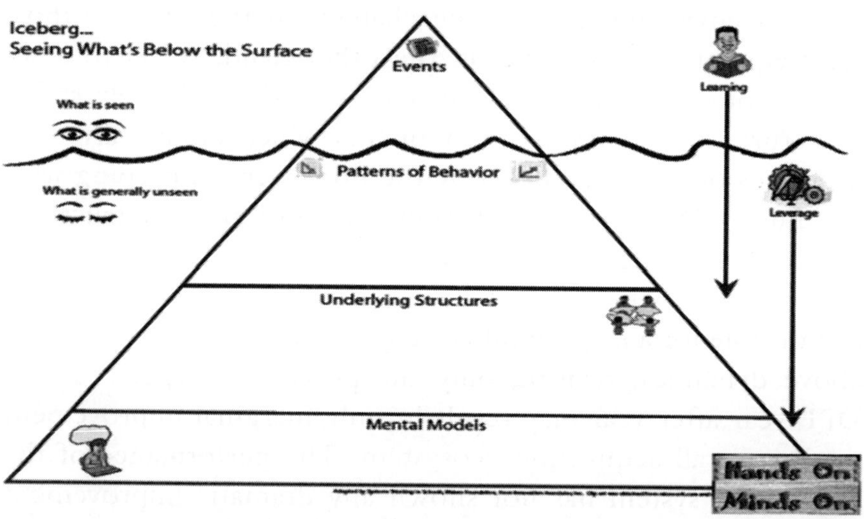

Study of the acquisition Task Responsibility Matrix (TRM) in defence capital acquisition divulges a multiplicity of agencies with overlapping roles working towards the deployment of a military capability, making the entire process more inefficient and ineffective[6]. The process starts from issue of the Raksha Mantri's Operational Directive (RMOD). The preparation of the Long-Term Integrated Perspective Plan (LTIPP) is the responsibility of the HQ IDS which is assigned the task to prepare the LTIPP, however, the MoD , MoD (Production) and MoD (Finance) remain in the consultative and informatory role, thereby prolonging the cycle. Similarly, the Services Capital Acquisition Plans (SCAPs), Annual Acquisition Plans (AAPs) and Technology Perspective Capability Roadmap (TPCR) are finally compiled by the IDS while the MoD remains in the consultative and informatory role. Similarly, for Acceptance of Necessity (AoN) and categorisation cases, the MoD still has an informatory and consultative role without accountability for the delay. A cursory glance at the various steps, of the acquisition system reveals that the SHQ shoulders the responsibility for negotiating numerous steps while the authority lies with the MoD, MoD (Production) and MoD (Finance) that jointly own the acquisition system.

Examining the Acquisition System Through SSM

The framework for classifying various methodologies for systems was developed by Jackson and Keys in 1984 and is referred to as the System of System Methodologies (SOSM). The participants are on the X axis and the systems are on the Y axis, as depicted in Table 4.1 below:

Table 4.1: Jackson and Keys Grid of Systems Theory

	UNITARY	PLURALIST	COERCIVE
SIMPLE	**Simple Unitary** Hard systems thinking, system dynamics, organisational cybernetics.	**Simple Pluralist** Soft system approaches.	**Simple Coercive** Emancipatory systems thinking and post-modern systems thinking.
COMPLEX	**Complex Unitary** Complexity theory.	**Complex Pluralist** Soft system approaches.	**Complex Coercive** Emancipatory systems thinking and post-modern systems thinking.

Simple systems are those having a few sub-systems that are involved in a small number of highly structured interactions. On the other hand, extremely complex systems have a large number of sub-systems that are involved in many more loosely structured interactions, the outcome of which is not pre-determined. Unitary participants have similar values, beliefs and interests, and share a common purpose. The military set-up is a typical example of a unitary system. In a pluralist relationship, although basic interests are compatible, they do not share common values and beliefs which is the case with the acquisition system. In coercive relationships, there are few common interests and participants hold conflicting values and beliefs. No agreed objectives direct the actions of coercive participants. The hard systems thinking falls in the category of simple unitary where mathematical and analytical models can be made applicable. However, as the complexity increases or where a pre-defined goal cannot be stated, the approach would become inadequate. Moving down the axis increases the complexity of the system and the number of variables becomes large, with a greater number of interactions, making mathematical modelling impossible due to the dynamics of the system and environment. In such cases, the system is analysed with the help of system dynamics. However, military systems are increasingly becoming complex human activity systems and, hence, the Soft Systems Methodology (SSM)[7] is required to be used to address them. The acquisition system falls in the category of a complex pluralist system. Each person's world view is a complex set of attitudes, beliefs, values, opinions and perceptions. In soft systems, the situation is perceived to exhibit crisis, conflict and uncertainty in relationships among the actors. SSM follows the undermentioned sequence:

- The *first step* involves understanding and expression of the unstructured situation by analytical tools like the rich picture.
- *The second step* involves culling out of relevant systems and their root definitions from the rich picture. A relevant system is one,

which is thought to be helpful in learning about situations. The relevant systems can be both issue-and primary task-based. The issue-based definitions are generally related to the mental process, whereas the primary task-based are operationalised. The root definitions are expressed as '*a system to do X by Y in order to achieve Z*'.

- *The third step* involves evolving a conceptual model using the relevant systems and their root definitions. The conceptual model is based on the desired transformation and includes monitoring and controlling elements. It also has design measures for the three criteria of efficacy, efficiency and effectiveness and, if required, ethics, as also gives out the hierarchy and connectedness of various activities.
- The *fourth step* involves comparing the activities of the conceptual models with real life existing situations. Any changes implemented should be both systematically desirable and culturally feasible.

Rich Picture Analysis: Accordingly, in keeping with the tenets of SSM, a rich picture, which has been constructed for the acquisition system, is examined, which gives the visual summary of the human activity system under discussion, i.e. the acquisition system. The rich picture has been obtained from various sources such as personal experiences of the author, memoranda of minutes, and stakeholder interviews. The analyst should be able to draw out a number of primary and secondary tasks and issues which seem important to the situation and have been listed in Fig 4.4 below.

Fig 4.4: Rich Picture of Acquisition System

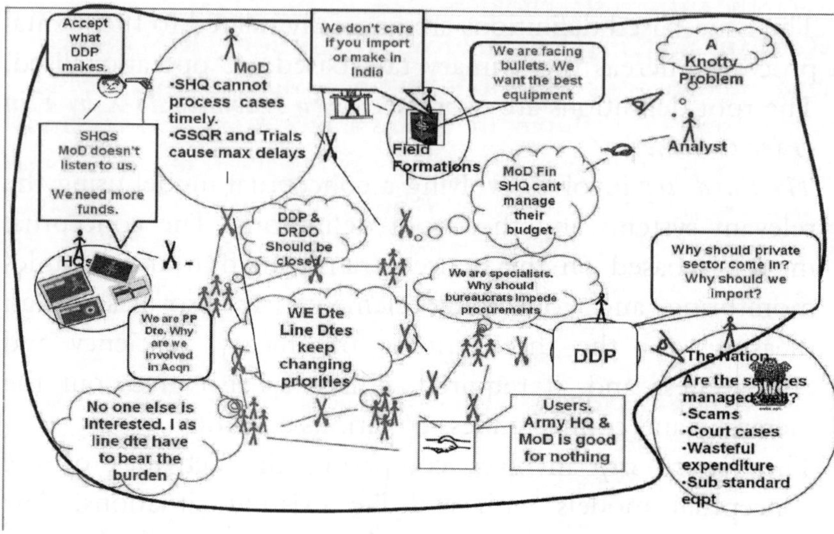

World Views of Stakeholders

- The SHQ believes that delays are caused at the MoD level and the bureaucracy is to blame for being unresponsive.
- End users want the best equipment and that too timely, whether it is 'Made in India' or ex-import.
- The MoD believes that the SHQ are not handling the priorities and budget correctly.

A two-fold analysis of the rich picture has been attempted to include both task-based and issue-based analysis. Task-based analysis of the rich picture depicts, *firstly*, that the primary task of the acquisition system is timely procurement within the approved budget. *Secondly*, the aim of self-reliance in defence equipment needs to be accorded primacy. *Thirdly*, the aspect of probity and public accountability should be central to any procurement. The issue-based analysis explains the issues impacting acquisitions viz *firstly*, the acquisition process is too long and time consuming; *secondly*, there are too many stakeholders and the organisation is too complex; *thirdly*, there is a perceptible lack of communication between the stakeholders; *fourthly*, there is a difference in opinion between the various stakeholders.

Relevant Systems (RS) and Root Definitions (RD): Relevant systems and their root definitions have been derived from the issue identified from the rich picture at this stage. A relevant system is one which is thought to be helpful in learning about the situations. The relevant systems can be both issue and task-based and the core of any relevant system is the transformation it performs. The root definition should pass the CATWOE (Customer, Actor, Transformation, Worldview, Owner. Environment) test which is a useful mnemonic for structuring root definition. Accordingly, the root definition for the acquisition system can be defined as an optimal acquisition system **TO** ensure timely acquisition of weapons and equipment within the desired budget **BY** realigning the structures and processes in the MoD **FOR** meeting the aspirations of the end user.

CATWOE Test:

- **Customer** – End users in Army units and formations.
- **Actors** – MoD, MoD (Fin), DDP, senior officers in field formations, DCOAS (P&S) DGs of Line Dtes, DG WE, DG PP, Army and other (civil and tri-Service) training institutions and PBOR (Personnel Below Officer Rank.
- **Transformation** – **FROM** the existing system devoid of accountability for time and cost over-runs **TO** a system closely monitored through suitable structures and processes.
- **Worldview** – Lack of suitable organisational structures and accountability in the existing stakeholders results in acquisition time and cost over-runs in acquisition.
- **Owner** - Ministry of Defence.
- **Environment** – Public and private sector, industry, Ministry of Commerce, Ministry of External Affairs.

Conceptual Model: Accordingly, a conceptual model for the acquisition system has been evolved which guides the analyst to the transformation desired in the system and has been shown in Fig. 4.5 below.

Fig. 4.5: Conceptual Model

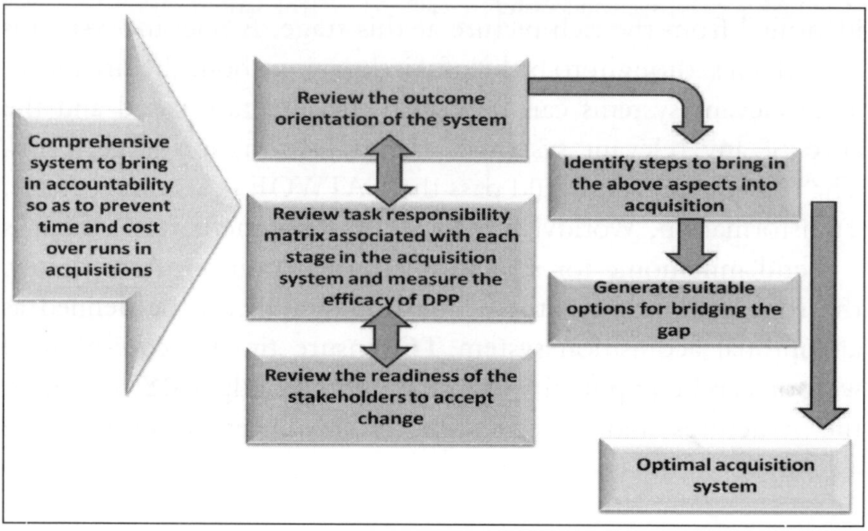

Comparison of Existing and Desired Systems: In keeping with the sequence of SSM discussed above, Table 4.2 below gives the comparison of various activities mandated by the conceptual models i.e. the process desired compared with that existing as on date. Such comparisons will generate ideas for change for further debate and implementation. In the case of the acquisition system under discussion, three main activities are evolved on examination of the conceptual model for improvement of the DPP along with the aspects that need emphasis in the form of back-up activities and observations. Analysis reveals that these activities do not figure in the existing acquisition system or the real world as elaborated in the 'observation' column of Table 4.2 and, hence, are required to be added to the agenda. These activities need to be reengineered to enhance the output of the acquisition system as a whole.

Table 4.2: Comparison of Existing Vs Desired Processes

Main Activity	Back-up Activity	Present in Real World	Observations	Add to Agenda
Review the task responsibility matrix with each stage in acquisition process and gauge the efficacy of the process.	Has the DPP been successful in reducing import dependence?	No	India remains the largest importer of arms in the world[8].	Yes
	Is the DPP effective as a capability-building document?	No	The DPP is largely a contract operating manual rather than a capability-building document. The Services remain devoid of critical capabilities[9].	Yes
	Has the DPP been successful in achieving the desired capability in the mandated timelines?	No	Acquisition timelines are violated in most acquisition cases.	Yes

Main Activity	Back-up Activity	Present in Real World	Observations	Add to Agenda
	Has the DPP been effective in establishing capability as per laid down QRs?	No	*Flawed GSQRs are responsible for more than half the cases being closed prior to delivery*[10]*. However, the capability being inducted finally conforms to the laid down QRs.*	Yes
	Has the DPP been effective in ensuring a high standard of probity and transparency?	No	*The acquisition system in India has been mired in a series of corruption cases in the recent past*[11]*.*	Yes
	Have continuous revisions of the DPP led to improvements in capability development and self-reliance?	No	*The DPP has undergone nine revisions, however, little capability enhancement has been seen as a result of these revisions,*[12] *while India remains low in self-reliance in defence*	Yes

Main Activity	Back-up Activity	Present in Real World	Observations	Add to Agenda
Review the outcome orientation of the acquisition system.	Need for timely establishment of capability and its conflict with other acquisition aims such as cost-effectiveness, self-sufficiency, probity and competition.	No	*Timely establishment of capability is often sacrificed in favour of propriety, probity, public accountability free competition and impartiality, as laid down in the aims of the DPP*[13].	Yes
	Does capability establishment have a defined ownership under the existing acquisition system?	No	There is no single owner of a particular acquisition case.	Yes
	Does the acquisition system facilitate adequate coordination between various stakeholders for capability establishment and its effect on self-reliance of defence needs?	No	*There is a lack of coordination between various stakeholders despite the agreement on the overall aim of achieving a capability*[14].	Yes

Main Activity	Back-up Activity	Present in Real World	Observations	Add to Agenda
	Does the acquisition system mandate application of programme management towards achieving of an acquisition outcome?	No	Presently, no significant project management techniques are being carried out in the field of acquisition, hence, its benefits are not clearly known to the environment.	Yes
	Does the acquisition system promote and foster processes and structures to build in inherent accountability?	No	Programme management needs to be built in to bring in accountability.	Yes
	Does the system promote a need for joint perspective planning?	No	*The Services, DRDO, and the industry need to plan jointly to achieve the aim of self-reliance in defence*[15].	Yes

Main Activity	Back-up Activity	Present in Real World	Observations	Add to Agenda
Review the readiness of stakeholders to accept change.	Is there a congruence of views in stakeholders towards timely establishment of military capability?	No	There is incongruence of world views among stakeholders towards timely acquisition of a capability.	Yes
	Is achievement of the desired outcome considered more important than achieving functional excellence in the individual sphere of stakeholders?	No	Presently, the emphasis is on coordinating the functional aspects rather than systemic excellence and the focus is output-based rather than outcome-based.	Yes
	Is there adequate effort to reduce the long-winded procedures in order to achieve timely establishment of capability?	No	The existing DPP consists of evaluations by multiple committees which are open- ended, causing delays, as a result of which it is very difficult to build in the required accountability into the system.	Yes

Main Activity	Back-up Activity	Present in Real World	Observations	Add to Agenda
	Is the appraisal system effective enough to facilitate achievement of both functional and systemic excellence?	No	*The appraisal system needs to be so designed that the functionary is able to operate in a matrix organisation and report to the functional as well as the programmme heads.*[16]	Yes
	Are adequate efforts being made to ensure infusion of the best IT and programme management practices to ensure the goals of defence procurement?	No	*Advanced Armies have implemented the best IT and programme management practices which the Indian system is still devoid of*[17].	Yes
	Are there adequate efforts to determine the role of leadership towards driving acquisition programmes?	No	The leadership needs to drive the programmes aggressively for timely acquisition of a capability.	Yes

The deductions arrived at through the systems approach have been discussed in Table 4.2 above, after which a primary research has also been undertaken by the author in order to substantiate these deductions. The sampling frame for the research consisted of 131 serving military and civilian officers dealing with acquisition in various capacities in the SHQ, MoD and DRDO as also officers of the National Defence College (NDC) course representing the users. Inputs were also sought from members of the corporate sector entities dealing in defence acquisition. A survey instrument based on the major issues flagged by the conceptual model was designed and responses sought from the various stakeholders as outlined above. The first aspect was devoted to measuring the attitudes of stakeholders towards the popular perception that a ***process*** revision, i.e. a revision of the DPP, will give an outcome orientation to the acquisition system. The responses were sought on a scale of 1 to 5, with 3 being neutral and 1 and 5 being strongly disagree and strongly agree respectively. Here the mean response of all 131 respondents was neutral at 2.93 i.e. the respondents were not sure of achieving the outcome orientation through improvement in the DPP alone. The next aspect was devoted to measuring the felt need for a management ***structure*** that has a project and outcome orientation. The mean response arrived at was at 3.72 indicating a strong agreement that there is a need for a structure that can support project and outcome orientation to the defence acquisition process. The last aspect was targeted to measure the ***readiness to change*** among the respondents. The mean response was at 4.03 which indicated strong agreement in support of change. The survey result conclusively substantiates the findings of the systems approach and indicates strong agreement among the target population towards realigning structures for project and outcome orientation. The structural changes being sought are in terms of a lean and agile programme-based fully accountable acquisition organisation. The existing procurement organisation consists of three specialist verticals of *acquisition*, *production* and *technology* where the flow of the specialist functional authority is presently top-down. A lateral integration of the specialist authority through an additional programme vertical is proposed to ensure that best practices in that specialist vertical are mandated through orders and guidelines to achieve the outcome desired as part of a specialist contribution to the project e.g. procurement, production and quality assurance to name a few. Establishment of such lateral linkages at the operational level would convert it to an effective matrix organisation[18].

The sub-optimal output generated by the capital acquisition system in India is not a result of a lack of any new category or an impeded industry capability. The stakeholder's incongruence resulting from a silo-based acquisition structure deployed to execute the policy has itself been significantly responsible for decapitating the system. In an absence of enabling structures, the DPP 2016, in its new albeit finite avatar of largely being a contract operating manual may not be able to fulfill the outcome expected of it. The DPP represents the internal lead time of the MoD towards award of a contract and the laid down timelines can only be adhered to if the structures are redefined to promote dynamic processes. A legislative solution on the lines of the Goldwater Nichols United States Department of Defence Reorganisation Act of 1986[19] needs to be tabled to implement meaningful structural reforms facilitating lateral integration as mandated by the 'systems' thinking.

Notes

1. Vikas Rohilla, "Are High Value Defence Procurements Only About Procedures?" *Defence Management Journal*, College of Defence Management, September 2011.
2. "Government Mulling Separate Set-up for Defence Acquisition: Manohar Parrikar", PTI, February 25, 2016, http://www.ndtv. com /india-news / government-mulling-separate-set-up-for-defence-acquisition-manohar-parrikar-1281225

3. "The 11 Laws of Systems Thinking and Stakeholder Engagement", https://thoughtexchange.com/the-11-laws-of-systems-thinking-and-stakeholder-engagement/. Accessed on October 09, 2015. Peter M. Senge, *The Fifth Discipline* (Doubleday/Currency, ISBN 0-385-26094-6, 1990).
4. George Wilhelm Fredrick Hegal (1770-1881), a pioneer in systems thinking, had propounded the postulate stating that the system as a whole has an objective which may not be explained by the parts. The study of the parts alone will not explain the whole system.
5. J W Forrester (1956), the founder of the concept of system dynamics, which employs the services of feedback to study complex , multi-layered, non-linear systems.
6. "Parrikar Finds $2.3 Billion Lying 'Forgotten' in US Account", PTI, *Hindustan Times*, March 05, 2016 http://www. hindustantimes. com/india/ parrikar-finds-2-3-billion-lying-forgotten-in-us-account/story- ydrldG 1bc9V8Uo8b PMW0FP.html
7. SSM was introduced by Peter Checkland in 1981.
8. Dinaker Peri, "India Retains the World's Largest Weapons Importer Tag", *The Hindu*, February 23, 2016, http://www.thehindu.com/ news / national / india-retains-worlds-largest-weapons-importer-tag/article8271899.ece
9. "Indian Army Grapples with Arms, Gear Shortage", February 28, 2016, http://timesofindia.indiatimes.com/india/Indian-Army-grapples-with-arms-gear-shortage/articleshow/51173589.cms
10. Lt Gen Philip Campose, PVSM, AVSM, VSM** (Retd), "Challenges to Modernisation", *Defence and Security Alert,* Vol. 7, Issue 4, January 2016.
11. Deba R Mohanty, "India's Defense Sector Still Plagued by Corruption", ISN, February 13, 2014, http://www.isn.ethz.ch/ Digital-Library/Articles/Detail/?lang=en&id=176507
12. Vivek Raghuvanshi, "India Plans Procurement Policy Revisions", *Defence News,* January 25, 2016, http:// www. defensenews.com /story/defense/policy-budget/industry/2016/01/25/india-plans-procurement-policy-revisions/79053214/
13. DPP 2013, Para 2, http://cgda.nic.in/pdf/DPP2013.pdf
14. "PM Chairs Combined Commanders Conference on Board INS *Vikramaditya* at Sea," Press Information Bureau, December 15, 2015, Prime Minister's Office, http://pib.nic.in/newsite/PrintRelease.aspx?relid=133265
15. Amol A. Gokhale, "Redefining DRDO to Create, Innovate and Make in India", January 04,2016, http://bharatshakti.in/ redefining-drdo-to-create- innovate-and-make-in-India/

16. "Review of Acquisition for the Secretary of State for Defence: An Independent Report by Bernard Gray", www.bipsolutions. com/docstore/ Review Acquisition Grayreport.pdf.
17. Ibid.
18. Research evidence suggests that an organisation that employs 3,000 employees is likely to have seven levels in its hierarchy and is a tall organisation. Unduly tall organisations suffer from major communication and motivation problems.
19. The Goldwater–Nichols Department of Defence Reorganisation Act of 1986 Pub.L. 99–433, signed by President Ronald Reagan, made the most sweeping changes to the United States Department of Defence since the department was established by the National Security Act of 1947, by reworking the command structure of the United States military.

5. PROGRAMME MANAGEMENT STRUCTURE FOR DEFENCE ACQUISITIONS: THE WAY FORWARD

In accordance with the provisions of DPP , the acquisition of weapon systems and equipment for the armed forces flows from the LTIPP over 15 years duration. The LTIPP is translated into specific assets to be acquired, in the form of the SCAP, covering a five-year period. A list of equipment and weapon systems required to be procured immediately is listed in the form of the AAP. The AAP covers a period of two years and rolls over to the next financial year, derived from the SCAP. The AAP is prepared and prioritised in consonance with the budget allocation for capital acquisitions. Presently, the AAP 2014-16 is in vogue and consists of schemes from the approved Army SCAP 2012-17. Presently, no project management is carried out in the acquisition in the Services except in the case of a 'Make' procedure where a loosely constituted IPMT has been prescribed in the DPP. However, till date, not a single substantial 'Make' case has fructified since its inception.

The Bernard Gray reforms to the acquisition system of the UK effected in 2009,[1] covered in great detail the entire spectrum from capability building to acquisition of equipment. The Bernard Gray Report specifically recommends that the delivery arm of the UK MoD i.e. the Defence Equipment and Support (DE&S) among others, needs greater levels of skills in programme and project management. The report brings out that the DE&S management structure lacks focus on the core area of project management for equipment procurement and support and that the organisation is not structured in the most suitable way to deliver a programme of Pounds 1.2 billion per annum on equipment procurement and support. The report says that the head of the project organisation for acquisition should have extensive experience in running project-based organisations of similar size and complexity. Enforcing such a requirement renders unlikely that such an individual could be recruited from within the armed forces. A similar review for the Australian Defence Force (ADF) was carried out in 2008 and later in 2015, which pointed at inadequate project management resources in the Capability Development Group (CDG) as one of its major concerns[2]. Project management the world over has been established and accepted as the only credible way for efficient capital acquisition which, unfortunately, finds no presence in the Indian system. Little wonder then, that the Indian system has failed to meet the aspirations of the users. In fact, all stages of the existing DPP are most amenable and can easily be aligned to a typical project as is also being followed in advanced Armies. Establishment of a defence capability can be broken into four phases *viz.* the *concept* phase, *planning* phase, *execution* phase and *transfer* phase which correspond to various phases of a typical project.

The apex of the current procurement structure implied by the DPP is the DAC headed by the RM and in which the RRM, Service Chiefs, all Secretaries of the MoD and the Deputy Chief of Integrated Defence Staff (DCIDS) are members. The body, akin to a company Board of Directors, holds significant strategic and financial authority vested in it. The three main functional verticals involved in the establishment of capability for the armed forces are the Defence Production Board controlling all DPSUs and OFB, the Research & Development (R&D) Board controlling the DRDO, and the Defence Procurement Board which encapsulates all specialist functions of the three Services and IDS required for carrying out procurements. The Defence Production Board owns the production function for indigenous and licensed builds, the R&D Board owns the National Defence Technology Roadmap and the procurement specialist functions viz contracts, commercial and technical or operational are owned by the Defence Procurement Board. This structure is a functional organisational structure with limited formal cross-functional interactions except when specifically called for by the DPP in the case of categorisation of proposals viz. SCAPCHC and SCAPCC. All project decisions are centralised at the organisational apex and the bandwidth available at that level would, therefore, be limited. A failure by one of the sister boards, i.e. Production Board or the R&D Board to deliver a capability on time is only resolved at the organisational apex with no cross-communication or collaborative problem solving at the functional level. The key point to note is that the organisational apex is ultimately responsible for any failure in the schedule or cost of establishment of a capability. This is in sync with the systems and statistical analysis carried out in Chapter 4 that there is a pressing need to formalise organisational structures that would own programme, portfolio and project management functions. Reorganisation of specialist functions within each functional vertical for each of the specialities i.e. land, sea and air systems would greatly help in developing groups of excellence for joint capability development structures as well as providing effective functional support to a projectised organisation through a project management vertical. The project management vertical is not an entirely new concept in the DPP which mandates Integrated Project Management Teams (IPMTs) in the ship-building guidelines and 'Make' procedure of the DPP. The IPMTs are cross-functional teams that are formed for the management of individual or small groups of homogenous projects. These teams typically function under the direct control of the programme management groups of each Service and are required to create project plans authorising detailed milestones to be met in a given timeframe.

The corporate sector in India is driving highly complex projects worth millions of dollars annually, using state-of-the-art technology and project management best practices. A typical multinational vertical with a single domain specialisation would be handling approximately 200 projects annually with an outlay of US $15 billion which roughly equals the Rafale deal. Any new project undertaken by a corporate entity in India today is first examined by an apex committee akin to a Project Initiation Forum (PIF). The PIF consists of subject matter experts from different verticals such as telecom, banking, finance, and media. The PIF accords the first pass to a project post initial risk analysis. DPP is also silent on risk management in all categories of acquisition except for a fleeting mention in the case of the 'Make' procedure. In capital acquisitions, there is a variety of external and internal risk factors that needs to be assessed. A precondition to overall risk management is risk assessment. Risk assessment involves analysing the probability, the impact, and the effect of every known risk on the achievement of established objectives, as well as the corrective action to be taken should that risk occur. Risk assessment is, therefore, a prerequisite for determining how the risks should be managed and mitigated. Mitigation seeks to put in place measures to lessen the severity of a risk event, should that event occur. To realise the maximum benefit of risk management, the management and communication of risks needs to be an integral part of existing procurement and organisational functions. Thereafter, the project is allotted to a programme manager rather than the domain specialist, hence, making the programme manager responsible for execution of a particular project from the very beginning. The programme manager, in turn, has a number of project managers under him and assigns this particular project to one of them. The project manager so detailed interacts with all the verticals required in the project, called the Delivery Project Executives (DPEs), and asks them to assign resources, namely, line function executives, to fulfill the project requirements. Line function executives are assigned by DPEs who also work out detailed time and cost estimates, detailed risk analysis and detailed requirements of resources. The second pass approval is accorded somewhere at this stage. These line function executives will report to the programme manager in addition to their vertical head, thus, ensuring a projectised organisation is in place. In case there is a risk of time and cost over-runs, the project manager will know the exact problem and will resolve it. If the resolution is beyond the project manager, the programme manager will be informed, who will interact with the senior delivery manager of the concerned vertical for resolution and the escalation loop continues till the risk is mitigated. Mid-course corrections are carried out by the project team as the project progresses and milestones are charted through inhouse software . These project management models are commonplace in India and seldom suffer time and cost over-runs and comprise the only way to enhance the effectiveness of the defence capital acquisitions in India.

Internationally, the capability development programme of the Australian Defence Forces (ADF) is an apt case study, identical to Indian conditions, as the ADF also sources a sizeable content of its high-tech weapon systems ex-import. Australia has one of the most evolved capability and acquisition management organisations in the form of the Capability Development Group (CDG) and the Defence Material Organisation (DMO). Capability planning in the ADF has a life cycle that begins with the shortfall between what the government wants the ADF to achieve and the capacity of the ADF. This is then progressively translated into a new capability system or an upgrade of the existing system. The ADF, on an annual basis, presents a submission developed by the CDG to the government, laying down the capability gap. The most concrete expression of the government priorities for development of the ADF is the Defence Capability Plan (DCP), which unlike the Indian LTIPP is a duly costed ten-year roll-on plan of the yet unapproved capital acquisition projects. Before a project is included in the DCP, it is clearly defined as to what the project will deliver, at what cost, and in what schedule, as also the initial risk inherent with the project. The CDG is responsible for informing the government of the capability, cost and schedule, and the risk inherent in each project so that the government can take an informed decision. Prior to seeking entry into the DCP, formal agreement is documented on the cost schedule and capability requirements of the project as well as the *acquisition strategy*. This agreement is signed by the chief of the CDG and the capability manager who is usually a Service Chief and CEO of the DMO. The ADF devotes 10 to 15 percent of its project funds for complex projects before the first pass for detailed analysis and project definition. Risk analysis in the beginning would benefit from the initial investment in terms of technical risks, integration and commercial risks. Thereafter, the capability is transformed into costed and defined requirements. The approval for acquisition of a capability is accorded by the government through a tailored *two pass* process which accords a greater rigour to high cost and technologically complex projects while simple projects are cleared in a lesser timeframe. In the first pass, funding for approved options is fully analysed through detailed studies, analyses and industry studies, and at this stage, no commitment is given by the government to acquire the capability. Care is taken that most of the capital acquisitions are carried out off the shelf as in their experience, setting requirements beyond those of "off the shelf" generates disproportionately large increases to cost, schedule and risk to projects. To facilitate accountability between stakeholders at this stage, namely the CDG and DMO, IPMTs are formed and a draft Material Acquisition Agreement (MAA) is developed which reflects the expected capability required by the capability managers and the business acquisition strategy developed by the DMO. The MAA ensures that all stakeholders understand their respective responsibilities throughout the acquisition. This results in the DMO achieving most of its projects before time. An unclassified version of the DCP is published every two years to inform the industry of the specific nature and size of each project. The DCP provides the description and background, likely acquisition strategy, through life support considerations, planned year of government decision and entry into service, anticipated cost range and opportunities for industry.

Capability-building in tune with defence requirements is a vital activity for any nation. Capability-building is typically carried out through induction of equipment and training of personnel of the armed forces. In order to ensure that capability-building is carried out in step with the NSS, the introduction of the DPP for capital procurements was an important step. The aim of the procedure was to ensure that no capability and, therefore, strategic gap was created between the nation and its threats by ad-hoc procurement practices which were followed up to that time.

Defence capital acquisition projects routinely fail and this phenomenon is not peculiar only to the Indian scenario. Instances of delayed acquisition projects due to time and cost over-runs are observed in procurement organisations the world over. These advanced Armies, when compared to India, have, however, evolved their 'capability definition and acquisition hierarchy' structures over the years which, unfortunately, are conspicuously absent from the Indian acquisition executive. If we were to examine two recent capital schemes pertaining to the Army's critical equipment, certain definitive failings will clearly emerge. The first of the two cases is that of the assault rifles where the Army scrapped a four-year-old tender for importing 1.8 lakh multi-calibre assault rifles in June 2015, retracting the INR 4,848 crore Request for Proposal (RFP) floated in 2011, thereby losing almost a decade of valuable time in replacing the under-performing INSAS rifle currently in use. The failure of this case can be ascribed to an inability in identifying apparent and estimable risks before fielding this case to the DAC. Going by the vast repository of aborted cases in the recent past, the failure of GSQRs in an ex-import procurement given the current 'Make in India' milieu, is an identifiable risk that should have been assessed and mitigated while fielding the case. The other important case involving a critical life saving albeit low technological equipment which even after half a decade eludes closure is that of the bullet-proof jackets. Acceptance of Necessity (AoN) for this case was accorded by the DAC in October 2009 with a envisaged capability deployment timeline of 2012. The RFP was, however, retracted due to GSQR related issues after a gap of more than two years and a fresh RFP could be issued only one year after it was retracted. The trials for this item reportedly commenced somewhere at the end of 2014 and this tender has been scrapped due to the reported failure of all six vendors to meet the GSQR parameters. Both these cases have failed due to lack of risk assessment in drawing up the GSQRs, categorisation and subsequent trials. Similarly, the grounds for cancellation of the contract for 197 utility helicopters after almost a decade of altercations before deciding to manufacture it in India, fall in the domain of 'strategic and commercial risks' which could have been mitigated had an adequate risk management exercise been carried out at the planning stage.

The 15-year LTIPP of capital equipment is the fountainhead based on which the Services are equipped post the DAC approval. Initial fielding of a capital scheme into the LTIPP and later to the DAC warrants due diligence in the present era of ever shrinking capital budgets. Inaccurate risk, cost and schedule estimates would lead to either a recast of the LTIPP or failure of cases at the procurement stage, as seen in the cases of the assault rifles and bullet-proof jackets, both provoking unwarranted criticism of the procurement executive. Therefore, the inclusion of a particular acquisition scheme into the LTIPP should be subject to an incisive analysis to facilitate greater clarity in terms of deliverables, a clearer evaluation of the intrinsic project risk, and a more accurate estimate of its cost and schedule on the basis of detailed research. Only by doing so will the DAC have the wherewithal necessary to take an informed decision for approving a particular scheme. A structure in the form of a CDG tasked to carry out risk, cost and schedule assessment and management before the first approval of the government needs to be put in place in India at the earliest.

Eighty-one capital schemes worth INR 1.5 lakh crore have been approved in principle by the DAC in the past two years since the present government came to power. However, it still takes about a decade for any capability envisaged through the DAC approvals to be physically deployed owing to slippages, time and cost over-runs. Recasting the LTIPP due to changed priorities and imprecise analysis is not uncommon and there are also instances where a number of old acquisition schemes are not rolled over from one LTPP to the other, citing their non-utility, thus, indicating a lack of rigour prior to its inclusion in the plan in the first place. No amount of procedural reform can offset the spin-offs that can accrue from the creation of a CDG. India presently has no structure in place which carries out an analysis from the risk cost and schedule points of view at any stage of procurement. Schemes are inserted in the LTPP based on an internal geo-strategic and technology scan by the Army HQ, augmented by inputs gathered from the lower formations, consequently bypassing a stringent capability analysis.

The Capability Development Executive (CDE) should be headed by a three-star armed forces officer of the status of Army Commander (or equivalent from the three Services; equivalent to a Secretary to the Government of India) called Commander-in-Chief Capability Development Executive (CINCCDE). He would report directly to the RM. At the apex level of the organisation, to assist the CINCCDE, there should be another Lieutenant General (or equivalent)/Additional Secretary level appointment dealing with integration, strategic prioritisation, budgeting and technology analysis, called Chief of Strategic Priorities (CoSP). The appointment should be on a rotational basis amongst the three Services as well as the civil services. At the execution level, Capability Development Groups (CDGs) will be formed under Lieutenant Generals/Major Generals or equivalent from the three Services who will be called Capability Development Managers (CDMs). To ensure joint development of capabilities, these will be formed on the basis of likely strategic environments for operations separately for China, Pakistan, Maritime Operations, UN Peace-Keeping Operations (PKOs), Air Operations, including Air Defence, Out of Area Contingency (OOAC) Operations, Counter-Insurgency/Counter-Terrorism (CI/CT) Operations, Net-Centric Warfare (NCW) Operations and Capability Integration Operations. The CDGs will be staffed by a mix of armed forces and civil service officers, including the three Services, Civil Services, Finance,

Costing, DRDO and DGQA. The Service officers should have domain knowledge of the respective fronts/operations being handled by the CDGs. The detailed composition of each CDG can be worked out subsequently once the broad outlines of such an organisation are approved, in principle. The organisation will also have an SQR Development Group (SQRDG) with an industry interface which will generate SQRs based on approved capability plans. This will address the lacuna in the system and aid in improving the process of development of SQRs. The tenure of appointments in the CDE should be long enough to ensure continuity and building up of institutional knowledge.

The CDG will perform the following functions. Firstly, the CDG will enhance the quality of the delivery of critical capability for the armed forces prior to its approval by the DAC through a 'top-down' flow based on the strategic guidance provided by the Raksha Mantri's Operational Directive (RMOD). Capability gaps will be arrived at through a comparison of the desired capabilities and assessment of the current capability. Feasibility studies would then lead to further fine-tuning of the desired capability after the financial, technological and industrial vetting by experts and integration and prioritisation by the capability managers. Secondly, the CDG will provide an assurance to the DAC that the funds have been spent in the national interest in conformity with the canons of financial propriety. Thirdly, the CDG shall prepare details of the capability required along with the initial data relating to cost, schedule and risk, developed by the relevant experts resourced within the CDG for this purpose. Fourthly, the CDG will communicate to the DAC a rigorous cost benefit analysis to benchmark all additional risks posed by fielding for procurement any equipment not available COTS. Lastly, the SQR Development Group, with an industry interface as a part of the CDG, will generate SQRs based on approved capability plans. This will address the lacuna in the system and aid in improving the process of development of SQRs.

Presently, there are many areas of concern, ranging from atrophied capability management and inadequate project management contributing to formulating an LTIPP generated through a bottom-up approach in the absence of an articulated National Security Strategy (NSS). Insufficiency of the process leading to DAC approvals for new projects and a fragmented silo-based acquisition structure are some other voids plaguing the acquisition system in India. While the Dhirendra Singh Committee Report on acquisition reform, building upon similar reports released over the last two decades, has recommended measures to deliver enhanced outcomes through a more corporatised acquisition organisation outside the structure of the MoD, the DPP versions promulgated till date do not, however, dwell in detail on the need for a structure akin to a CDG to address the planning aspect before actual procurement is affected.

To achieve its aim, the CDG will, *firstly,* need to be resourced with niche skills such as project planning and management in order to define a capability. The performance of the CDG shall impact greatly the later stages of acquisition and, hence, project management skills during the early stages of an acquisition are vital. Currently, the core Human Rights (HR) personnel staffing the perspective planning departments comprise Service officers on moderate tenures averaging 18 to 24 months serving in a highly complex domain. Planning and execution of complex military projects by Service officers with little or no proficiency in project management skills is not a practical option and needs reform. *Secondly*, the CDG shall also be responsible for working out the life cycle costs for material as well as non-material capabilities allied to the procurement case such as training of personnel, infrastructure development, etc, for which it will need to possess integral cost estimation expertise. *Thirdly*, the CDG will have to allocate increased resources devoted to the area of research and analysis which is a prime source for obtaining cogent information on risk, costs and schedules, as well as commercial inputs on procurement options. *Fourthly*, investment, in terms of risk analysis would greatly benefit mitigation of both technological, commercial and other project related risks. Lastly, to sustain the above resources, allocation of a minimum 10 percent of the total project expenditure needs to be made to enable a detailed analysis prior to DAC approval of a project, which is presently not being done.

The process of capability development will be a 'top-down' flow, based on the strategic guidance provided by the RMOD. It would take into account budgetary constraints, except for some requirements which cannot be compromised whatever the cost (which must be spelt out in the Capability Development Plan - CDP). Also, this may be the first step towards the T1-L1 concept as acquisitions must be based on a mix of Best Capability (Technical-T1) and Economy (L1 or Lowest Cost). This would entail initially arriving at a statement of desired capability *vis-a-vis* assessment of current capability. Thereafter, the capability gaps would be identified and feasibility studies would be required to be carried out for defining capability development needs. The capability development plan will be finalised by each CDG, with financial, technological and industrial vetting by experts. Thereafter, the capability will be integrated and prioritised under the CoSP and thereafter it will be approved by the CINCCDE who will further process it for approval by the RM. Once the capability plans and SQRs are developed, the material aspects are processed for acquisition as prevalent now as per the DPP through the 15-years capability roadmap, DCAP and AAP. The non-material aspects of capability development such as organisational issues, training, personnel management, infrastructure development, logistics, etc will be undertaken by the respective Service HQ and IDS.

As discussed in the previous chapters, defence capital acquisition is a system and not simply a process. Modernisation of defence forces is dependent on the ability of a nation to build its capability and is a direct result of capital acquisition practices . Studies of organisational best practices to improve effectiveness suggest three focus areas viz structure, process and people. So far, most attempts have been undertaken by addressing only the DPP. In the current research, as discussed in the previous chapters, the following have been studied through the prism of the systems view.

- **Process**: What ails the system as far as the acquisition practices are concerned because of which the stated intent of the DPP is not being achieved?
- **Structure**: Is the existing procurement organisational structure to ensure public accountability, transparency in operations, impartiality and self- reliance?
- **People**: The people dimension has been addressed to the extent of change management implications due to a change in organisational structure.

Planning vs Budgeting. The armed forces carry out their planning and obtain AoNs for as many schemes as desired with an indicative budget. There is no indication from the budgeting point of view that each AoN will result in enhancement of combat capability on the ground. No prioritisation is accorded to the AoN by the armed forces either based on budgetary resources / changed strategic priorities. To take an example, AoNs worth INR 1,17,830 stand approved for 2014-15;[3] however, the entire modernisation budget for 2014-15 was INR 75,148, including 85-96 percent of committed liabilities. Hence, there is a mismatch amongst planning, budgeting and acquisition.

The defence planning and budgeting processes are currently independent of each other. The armed forces are free to plan and obtain AoNs for as many schemes as desired as long as the GSQRs are in place. There is, however, no assurance from a budgeting point of view that each AoN will result in a contract, programme and, capability on the ground. Similarly, the armed forces are under no obligation to reevaluate their proposal to examine the art of the possible and evaluate potential strategic gaps based on the budgetary commitment. Indeed, the armed forces do not even have to prioritise their proposals and all pending AoNs could potentially be considered as priority “one”, thereby confusing budget allocation. Budget allocation of all pending schemes will almost certainly blow a strategic monetary hole in the nation's finances that should ideally be a cause of concern for the military planners. This situation results in a continuously growing gap between desired capabilities and budgetary commitments, eventually making the planning process irrelevant. This situation can be reversed if strategy drives planning, planning drives programmes, programmes drive budgets and, finally, stringent programme management ensures that capabilities are delivered on time and within the budget every time. This, in management parlance, is called the Programme, Planning, Budgeting and Executon (PPBE) process.

PPBE Process: Providing programme traceability to the overall military strategy for each programme is typically achieved by adopting the PPBE system. PPBE will serve to integrate the strategy, programme, financial planning and execution. A brief description of the PPBE process is given below:

- **Planning:** The planning phase of PPBE begins with the articulation of resource-informed national defence policies and military strategy by the strategic leadership. This articulation is referred to here as the SDPG. This could be an elaborated document based on an evaluation of the threat perception thought a formal net assessment, which is continually monitored and refined through a strategic management process. This articulation is an essential part of the defence acquisition process and is the root document for the acquisition process.
- **Programming:** Typically, an organisation such as the COSC links the planning and programming phases of the PPBE process. The programming phase begins with each armed force, defence manufacturing unit and defence research agency writing a document usually named the Programme Objective Memorandum (POM) for each proposed programme that meets the strategic objective. The POM, when complete, will provide in detail the proposed budget (manpower and funding) for a typical period of five years. This document must also describe what is not fully funded, and the risk associated

with the budget shortfall for review by the strategic leadership. Metrics for programme success to enable effective monitoring and control of the programme are also developed during this phase. Marginal budget adjustment and potential strategic alternatives can then be chosen by the leadership (COSC) to integrate POMs from various agencies into an overall coherent defence programme. Unresolved issues can be raised upto the level of the Defence Secretary for closure allowing the finalisation of what is usually referred to as a Programme Decision Memorandum (PDM) which has the same horizon as the SCAP. This document will provide the overall plan of action for a five-year period detailing all aspects of manpower, functioning, and funding for this period.

- **Budgeting:** The budgeting phase is concurrent with the programming phase. Each Service, manufacturing unit and defence research agency submits its budget estimate with its Programme Objective Memorandum (POM). The Integrated Defence Staff then converts their programme budgets into a demand for grant along with justification. Typically, the budget forecasts for only the next two years, but with more details than the POM. These suggestions are reviewed by analyses from the Finance Ministry, C&AG, etc to ensure that programme funding matches the current policy, that the prices are right, and justified to the Parliament. Typically, the analyses would write-up their questions during the formal budget review hearings. After the hearings, each analyst prepares a Programme Budget Decision (PBD) for each programme that proposes financial adjustment to address any issue or problem identified during the hearing. The programme budget decision is then approved by a competent authority such as the Raksha Mantri and the updated capital budget request to Parliament is then finalised.
- **Execution**: DPP 2016, if reworked with the removal of the acceptance of necessity (which becomes redundant with the PPBE), would become an ideal document that describes the execution phase. This phase will start with the request for

proposal and end with the successful completion of the entry into service phase of the capability. The primary objective of this phase is to ensure that the desired capability is delivered according to the approved programme cost and timelines. The phase is punctuated by constant reviews wherein the metrics developed through the programming phase help measure actual output versus expected performance. If the programme misses its metrics, then the execution review may lead to recommendations to adjust the budget or programme so that it meets the desired outcomes. For this reason, the execution review of all ongoing programmes is carried out concurrently with the programme and budget review for new and proposed programmes.

Monitoring Metrics and Technology: An important adage in project management is, "if it cannot be measured, it cannot be managed". Therefore, measurement of activities needs to be mandated in any process. Effectiveness implies that the outcome of the process was successful at a strategic/macro level. Efficiency implies that the output of the process was efficiently achieved in terms of resources and time at a tactical level. Therefore, both strategic and tactical metrics will be necessary.

Strategic Metrics: Strategic metrics are historical in nature and are vital to steer ongoing acquisition projects. Acquisition of a weapon system, for instance, might have occurred within cost and on schedule but may end up being completely ineffective in achieving the original strategic goals. It is very important that the causes that resulted in such a situation are fixed and not repeated. It needs no emphasis that such qualitative metrics are not whitewashed for reasons of personal careers. This aspect is covered in the people section subsequently.

Tactical Metrics and Technology: Tactical metrics are those that are monitored during the execution of the project. These are the kind of metrics that project, programme and portfolio managers report about to a project management vertical within an organisation. These metrics are integrated into the work and cash flow of a project and are available on a networked metrics, and the technology is beyond the scope of this report. Some tactical metrics are summarised in the table below:

Table 5.1: Tactical Metrics Used to Monitor Project Execution

Tactical Metric	Question Answered	Measured
Time	How are we doing against the schedule?	Schedule Performance Index (SPI) = Earned Value + Planned Value.
Cost	How are we doing against the budget?	Cost Performance Index (CPI) = Earned Value + Actual Cost.
Resources	Are we within anticipated limits of resources spent?	Actual resource utilisation vis-a`-vis planned.
Scope	Have the scope changes been more than expected/	Number of change requests.
Quality	Are the quality problems being fixed?	Number of defects fixed per user acceptance test.
Action	Are we keeping up with our action item list?	Number of action items behind schedule for resolution.

Currently, the DPP is the sole process document that steers defence procurement. Analysts have flagged six main issues from time to time which are considered as problem areas with the acquisition system. *Firstly*, there is a growing trend of large value capital acquisitions that completely bypass the main procedure of the DPP through the inter-governmental agreement (Clause 71-72) and Foreign Military Sales (FMS) routes that have been pointed out as a sign of ineffectiveness of the DPP to achieve the necessary capability build-up in the desired timeframes. *Secondly*, there are currently eleven phases of evaluation that are carried out by no less than seven committees and 13 departmental organs between the SQR and post contract management stages. Seven of these phases have no time limits. *Thirdly*, there is a class division among industries created through categorisation such as foreign, Indian majors, state owned industries, Indian owned private industry, SMEs, etc. There has been a call for a level playing field. *Fourthly*, the offsets policy has been a non-starter when looked at from the point of view of its original intention, which is building indigenous capacity. Now the expanded scope is expected to have its own inter-ministerial issues when implemented on the ground without an agreed roadmap. We have had very little ToT for critical systems as a consequence of the existing provisions of the DPP. The last and the most important issue, which has the potential to resolve all others, is the lack of alignment of intentions of the DPP with the structure of execution and the lack of accountability to capability/ development. It is felt that there is a strong need to focus on this aspect more in order to bring in accountability into the DPP.

The aspect of mismatch of alignment between the intent of the DPP and the execution structure is given as under:[4]

- Statement of Intention.
- Improvement in Accountability.
- Refinement in Structure.

Statement of Intention

Intention of the DPP: The SDPG is a document derived from the National Military Strategy. This document provides the necessary guidance for the creation of the LTIPP, the five-year SCAP and the annual roll-on AAP. It is imperative that these plans achieve their procurement targets so that the overall capability outcome desired by the SDPG is achieved. It needs no emphasis that defence capability is a composite of the industrial, operational and technological capabilities of the nation.

Defence Technology Capability Roadmap: There is no substitute to self-reliance in key military technologies which enable the unhindered growth of indigenous defence technology capability. The intention of offsets is to eventually gain self-reliance through reverse investments from foreign vendors. Foreign vendors are unlikely to part with key technologies without sustained negotiations from own side. The requirement of a roadmap to provide the necessary guidance to achieve technology capabilities is, therefore, implied in the DPP though not explicitly stated.

Industrial Self-Reliance Roadmap: Another aim of the offsets provision is to build the industrial capacity for self-reliance in defence production. The requirement, therefore, to achieve defence manufacturing self-reliance through planned capacity build-up is also implicit in the DPP. Perspective plans for the industry and DRDO need to be in sync with the LTIPP in order to achieve the timelines specified in the LTIPP for almost all categories of procurement. The plans of the industry, armed forces and DRDO need to satisfy an outcome that is desired by the strategic apex of the MoD, which could be the DAC. This outcome would need to be in sync with the SDPG issued by a political body such as the CCS in order to be in sync with the developments in other state security apparatuses outside the MoD. Therefore, if the DPP is to achieve the aims that it has set for itself, it needs to transform itself into a procedure that will ensure that the integrated defence capability build-up plan for the nation is achieved for the desired capabilities within the desired timeframes. The plans need to be top driven to be effective and the LTIPP has to become the core operating document that would ensure that all plans are moving in sync. This top-down process is crucial for the effectiveness of the DPP and needs to be enshrined in the DPP with clear responsibilities of who will do what. The DPP is currently not explicit about the agencies responsible to determine capabilities or specifying timeframes for achieving those capabilities on the ground although these have been largely undertaken by the SHQ. Hence, the DPP should include text that requires the military capability roadmap (LTIPP), the defence technology capability roadmap/equivalent document and the industrial self-reliance roadmap/equivalent document to be in alignment with the SDPG or equivalent document. Secondly, the DPP must include text that requires the various departments of defence to create execution plans/processes/structures to ensure that the timelines and milestones required by the approved roadmaps for capability build-up for defence, technology and industry are achieved. Causes for delays must be escalated to the higher levels till resolution is achieved.

Improvement in Accountability

Capability Establishment Phases (C,D,E,F): Establishment of defence capability can be divided into four phases viz:

- **Concept Phase(C):** Operational and maintenance specialists, based on their experience, conceive a potential weapon system, based on possibilities and sustainability. The operational component envisages the various possibilities of employment to satisfy itself that the originally desired capability is actually achieved. The maintenance specialty would make an initial feasibility evaluation of the sustenance and availability aspects of potential weapon systems. This stage typically is completed with the acceptance of necessity of the system to establish the new capability and commencement of the process which will lead up to the award of the contract.
- **Planning Phase(D):** In this phase, the creation of the systems requirements specifications, the contractual framework for deliveries and the commercial process for enabling the activity are developed. Short-listing of potential vendors/equipment, trial evaluations, evaluation of design proposals, evaluation of manufacturing plans, evaluation/negotiation of commercial proposals and the award of contract to the most appropriate vendor are carried out at this stage.
- **Execution Phase(E):** This is the stage in which all parties to the contract fulfill their obligations and the deliverables accrue to the recipient Service.
- **Transfer Phase(F):** The transfer phase is the phase in which the delivered system is stabilised and the required systems of sustenance of the system to establish the desired capability are fully established.

Project Management: The four-stage endeavour described above, that aims to deliver a capability to the armed forces, can be stated to be a project, and a portfolio of such projects can be termed a programme. Project management is the discipline of planning, organising, securing, managing, leading, and controlling resources to achieve the specific goal of the endeavour. This management/leadership activity is interwoven into the four-stage process and the process is deeply dependent on the project management leadership for success.

A combined graphic showing the project phases, the effort required, the contractual stages and the main specialist functions in each phase that eventually lead up to the establishment of a desired capability, is placed below (Fig 5.1):

Fig 5.1: Capability Establishment Phases

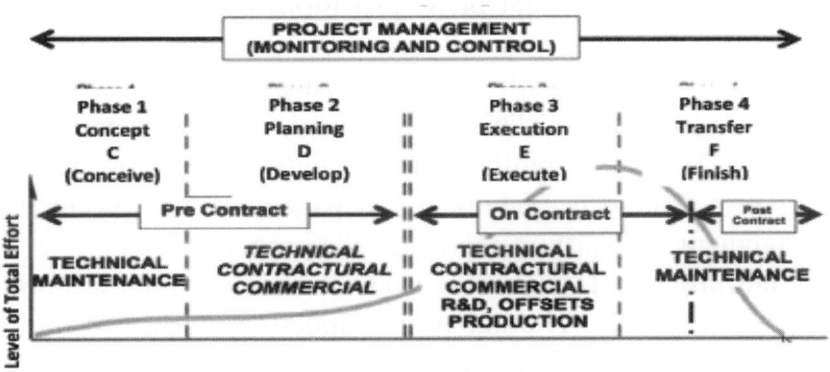

Phase 1	Phase 2	Phase 3	Phase 4
Concept	Planning	Execution	Transfer
C	D	E	F
(Conceive)	(Develop)	(Execute)	(Finish)

Project Phases/Functions and Roles Defined in the DPP: The project phases (including monitoring and control, which is a contiguous phase) have different functions which predominate in their contribution for successful completion of the phase.

Concept Phase: The technical and maintenance (sustenance) functions have a key role in the concept phase. Key DPP milestones that are achieved in this phase are finalisation of SQRs, accordance of the AoN and floating of the RFI/RFP. These specialist functions are typically performed by the SHQ, spearheaded by the Deputy Chiefs through teams of Service officers interfaced with the MoD through the Defence Acquisition Wing (AM, FM, TM). To a limited extent, the production function in the form of PSUs and OFB, DRDO and DOMW (Defence Offsets Management Wing) participate in the creation of a Technical Project Report (TPR) under the chairmanship of the Defence Acquisition Wing. This project report, however, is usually aimed at coordinating the finer details of technical specifications in order to ensure producability by the production function and alignment of offset proposals to the technology roadmap, if any. It, therefore, emerges from an assessment of the concept phase provisions of the DPP that the approvals for various specialist decisions are at the apex level i.e the DAC, and CCS, with no traditional programme managerial functions other than the limited coordination currently performed by HQ IDS, and currently, there is limited or no contribution of quality assurance, technology management and production management specialists at this stage of a proposal.

Planning and Design Stage: This is the stage the leads up to the contract award. The key project milestones achieved during this phase are the technical evaluation, field evaluation and staff evaluation of the various proposals received from the vendor at the end of the previous stage i.e initiation/conception stage. Depending on the size of the project, various guidelines for award of categorisation of the project, evaluations and commercial negotiations are provided by the DPP. The various specialist functions under the Defence Acquisition Wing (DAW) i.e. Acquisitions Manager (Contracts Function), Technical Manager (Operational Function), Financial Manager (Commercial Function) are closely assisted by the concerned specialists in the SHQ, typically spearheaded by the Deputy Chiefs of the three Services. Joint cross-functional committees such as the SCAPCHC and SCAPCC are catered for in the DPP for categorisation and acquisition process definition for equipment. In-Service structures, typically under the Deputy Chiefs, to finalise Joint Staff and General Staff Qualitative Requirements are left to the SHQ. The committee of the IHQ of the MoD (Army) such as the GSEPC (General Staff Equipment Policy Committee) and the JSEPC (Joint Staff Equipment Policy Committee), are examples of internal cross-functional structures that aid in the formulation of the SQRs. It emerges from the assessment of the planning and design phase provisions of the DPP that, as in the previous phase, the approvals for various specialist decisions are at the apex level i.e the DAC, CCS, with no traditional programme managerial functions other than the limited coordination currently performed by the HQ IDS. Secondly, there is limited or no contribution of quality assurance specialists at this stage of a proposal, and, thirdly, the maintenance management function is conspicuous by its absence at this stage. This function is crucial to ensuring in-service sustainability planning for the inducted capability. This centralised function would typically manage the establishment of maintenance capability with both Service and industry-based options for the echelons of maintenance above the operational level. This function will also need to consolidate the stocking policy and infrastructure to ensure smooth induction and establishment of the fleet.[5]

The Execution Phase: This phase commences with the award of contract and finishes with the receipt of all contractual deliverables. While shown as a discrete phase, this phase usually telescopes into the closure phase as deliverables to the recipient Service may be spaced in time and closure may happen simultaneously in respect of certain deliverables, while others may still be under production/ delivery, according to a mutually agreed programme. Any design and development of systems or production tools, their productionisation, production and delivery takes place during this phase. If produced indigenously, the PSUs and OFB play a major role and quality assurance is monitored by the DGQA and its equivalents for airborne and maritime systems. In pursuant of an offset agreement,

DOMW would facilitate delivery of any production technology to indigenous industry, while DRDO would manage technology induction into its fold if provided for in that manner in the offset agreement. It emerges from an assessment of the execution phase provisions of the DPP that the DPP, as in the previous phases, does not recognise the need for a suitably empowered formal programme management structure to ensure that the deliverables reach the recipient Service/other organisations involved, in accordance with the contract, and, secondly, the arrangement assumes that the contractual obligations would be completely satisfied by both internal and external contractors, and the protective clauses in the standard contractual document would be adequate to ensure that the capability is established in time.

Closure Phase: The closure phase is an important phase in which all necessary actions i.e. both contractual and non-contractual, to ensure the operational and maintenance capability establishment for sustenance of the weapon system are taken. This function is presently being performed by the MGOs branch. A project team typically spearheads this, with each specialist function confirming that the contractor has achieved contractual deliverables and contractual payments have been completed. It emerges that the DPP currently does not explicitly address this aspect. The DPP could be further refined to include a formal empowered project management structure to ensure that all stages of the capability establishment project are successfully achieved within the designated timelines and within the budget.

Project Hierarchy: The hierarchy of projects in an integrated defence capability build-up programme is enumerated below.

- **Project Level (Lowest)**: A large number of land, maritime and aerospace projects managed by individual project managers.
- **Portfolio Level**: A group of such projects that may achieve a lower level capability outcome can be considered as a single portfolio and a number of such programmes of projects would be managed by portfolio managers.
- **Programme Level**: All projects that roll out a composite land,

air or maritime capability can be considered as programmes and would be managed by programme managers.

- **Sponsor Level (Highest Level)**: The amalgamated outcome of these programmes would be the defence capability at any given time and would be typically managed by the programme sponsor, such as the DAC.

At all levels, the focus is on just three things "Schedule", "Quality" and "Cost".

Refinement in Structure: The apex of the current procurement structure has been discussed at length in the previous chapters and comprises three silos of procurements, production and R&D. As we have seen earlier, every project has four phases viz. initiation, planning, execution and closure. A project needs different specialist functions to be performed at different stages, as enumerated below:

- The procurement function is an important specialist function, which is currently spearheaded by the DG Acquisitions vertical in the MoD. The contractual (Acquisition Managers), commercial (Financial Managers), technical (Technical Managers) and sustenance (Maintenance Managers) aspects of an acquisition are addressed by sub-specialist verticals within the procurement vertical.
- The manufacturing function, currently spearheaded by the defence production vertical in the MoD, would be responsible for all aspects requiring manufacturing support in the establishment of the desired defence capability. Quality control is an important sub-specialisation of this vertical that ensures that the desired quality requirements are met by the manufacturing processes.
- The R&D function, which is led by the defence research vertical of the MoD, would be responsible for all aspects that require development of new systems and equipment through defence research. This vertical is the key to achieving self-reliance. Among the many sub-vertical specialisations within this vertical an important vertical is the productionising speciality, which transfers any newly developed system to the manufacturing function.

The flow of specialist functional authority is top-down in all the specialist verticals. The flow of specialist authority ensures that best practices in that specialist vertical are mandated through orders and guidelines to achieve the end result desired as part of a specialist contribution to a project. Costing and estimating functions are typically embedded into specialist functions of a large scale.

Project Vertical and Specialist Interface: It can be argued that project management is also a speciality. Best practices to ensure achievement of outcomes are embedded into the project management vertical through orders and guidelines in a manner very similar to that of the other verticals. However, a key difference in this vertical is its interface with specialist verticals. A project management vertical knits the specialists into a functional team, thereby, achieving the desired outcome of the project. The interface of this vertical with the specialist vertical is lateral and project authority flows laterally across the specialist verticals. The project management vertical takes complete responsibility for the project outcome while the functional verticals take responsibility for the project outputs. This type of organisation is called a *matrix organisation* or a two-dimensional organisation and is widely used for both military and civilian applications. Clearly, this feature is not present in the currently specified procurement organisation and, therefore, accountability for project outcomes is not specified. This is considered a major lacuna in the structure of the procurement organisation specified in the DPP which lays down responsibility for outputs but not for outcomes.

Projectised Organisations: Projectised organisations, popularly also called matrix organisations, have a two-dimensional structure. Examples of such organisations in operation are the DMO of Australia, the US' Homeland Security (after reorganisation post 9/11), DGA of the France, and the South African armed forces. The CDS/Theatre Command structure being considered for the Indian armed forces would also eventually be a good example of a matrix organisation. The first dimension of the two-dimensional matrix organisation is the traditional functional organisation where each speciality is organised in accordance with its functional specification, similar to the existing organisational structure for procurement dictated by the DPP. The second dimension is the project dimension, which takes responsibility for delivering a single cross-functional project within a specified schedule and cost. This dimension is assigned specialists from the functional verticals who act as resources for the project manager.

Integrated Project Management Teams: IPMTs are already in use in the ship-building guidelines of the DPP as well as the 'Make' procedure. IPMTs are cross-functional teams that are formed for management of individual or small groups of projects, which are of similar nature. These teams typically function under the direct control of the programme management groups of each Service. These teams are required to create project plans, which have detailed milestones to be met. The IPMT will steer the individual projects to completion in respect of the process requirements laid out in this procedure. It should have the powers to release payments in accordance with agreed payment terms in relation to achievement of milestones. Payment terms involving earned value are typically used by these teams to comprehensively monitor milestones and, in some countries, it is mandatory to release payments according to achieved milestones, called Earned Value Management (EVM). EVM also provides a good insight into the costing processes of the project and should be mandatorily used in respect of Indian vendors and PSUs.[6]

Previous analysis brings out two main areas of improvement possible to the procurement organisation implied by the DPP. These are, firstly, introduction of the programme management functionality in the existing acquisition structure and leveraging available expertise in the form of groups of excellence for land, maritime and airborne capability. Secondly, use of project management software to monitor the various activities and stages in the acquisition process to prevent time and cost over-runs.

Way Ahead

The pace of modernisation and military acquisition is a matter of concern not only for the Services but for the country as a whole. While issues like probity and public accountability are of critical importance, they can't become ends by themselves or be the principal roadblocks in the way of operational deliverance. As complexities in acquisitions increase, there will be a need for more innovation and multi-disciplinary involvement. Real time monitoring and total automation of the procurement process are, thus, the need of the hour. The recommendations on project management suggested here can provide the right impetus in achieving these objectives and are considered steps in the right direction. It is recommended that the project management vertical in the form of any of the options given below be instituted in the acquisition structure.

Option I – Capability Programme Board: An entirely new programme management vertical, which can be named as the "Capability Programme Board", is proposed in this option. This programme management vertical is an empowered team of portfolio and programme managers for land, air and maritime programmes, as mentioned earlier and is solely responsible for achieving the project outcome through the lateral flow of the project authority. The specialist verticals are responsible for achieving individual outputs as required by the project plan. The rank structure of this vertical is similar to the other verticals and could be an entirely civilian controlled vertical or a combination of civilian and military control which are indicated as sub-option A and sub-option B. The Capability Programme Board could be headed by the RRM. All Secretaries to the MoD and the Service Chiefs could be board members. This board will shoulder the turnkey responsibility for establishing the capability as defined in the LTIPP. The DG programmes would be what would technically be called the system owner for the programmes of the three Services. These programmes would be composite programmes, including the LTIPP, SCAP and AAP, technology roadmap and industrial roadmap. Programme and portfolio managers will be empowered to make financial and technical decisions. The specialists, as well as the project management, will be resourced from the traditional functional verticals. The performance reporting for team functionaries will be defined within the matrix structure in respect of both professional and project outputs. The board would have a Secretary level officer at the apex level, with programme managers for land, maritime and air systems at the next level. The various project managers and portfolio managers would operate below this level for individual projects. They would be resourced from the various specialist verticals. As mentioned earlier, a good example of the type of organisation presented in Option I is the Australian Defence Material Organisation (DMO). The key features of this organisation are the existence of a separate programme vertical, centres of excellence for systems and commercial aspects within the procurement organisation. Both civilian and military officers man the organisation. Today, the DMO handles approximately 300 major and minor acquisition and sustainment projects, with an annual budget of US$ 10-12 billion.[7]

Option II: Enhanced Defence Acquisition Wing (DAW): The structure with the Capability Programme Board presented as Option I is the ideal structure wherein there is no confluence/ conflict of functional and programme verticals till the board level. This is the traditional way of organising programme structures, as seen from the example of the Australian DMO. However, the challenge of change management may be too high to directly attempt an independent project organisation with no conflict/ confluence with functional verticals. Additionally, the level of specialisation of the civilian bureaucracy in military matters tends to be higher in the advanced countries and the model needs to be more realistic in the Indian context. An organisational structure that may be easier to achieve in the interim is what is proposed as the enhanced defence acquisition wing option. The only disadvantage of this option is the conflict/confluence of functional and project chains at the DG Acquisition level. This conflict may eventually act as a trigger to separate the programme function under a separate Secretary level officer at the MoD. The two essential differences from the earlier model are that the DG Acquisition gets augmented with a programme wing headed by DCIDS(PP&FD) in addition to his existing specialist infrastructure in the form of the acquisition wing. The internal reorganisation of other specialist functions into groups of excellence alluded to in the previous model continues to be relevant in this model as well. It is, thus, apparent that the introduction of the project management vertical, reorganisation of specialist functions as land, air and maritime centres of excellence for the given function, and introduction of a maintenance management function in the DAW would go a long way in ensuring that projects would be delivered on time, within the budget and to specification, to achieve the overall outcome of joint capability development of the armed forces in accordance with the vision of the LTIPP derived from the SDPG issued by the strategic apex of the nation.

Defence procurement is a complex and specialised field that requires stability, expertise, domain knowledge, including of legal aspects, and more than anything else, continuous monitoring and follow-up to ensure that the interconnected actions are carried out in time. Over the years, the DPP has evolved and achieved a definite shape. Nevertheless, it is a continuing process and, therefore, there is scope for further refinement and amendments in the days to come. Notwithstanding these guidelines, the defence capital procurements have far exceeded their time limits and today, no major procurement has materialised before seven to eight years. With India becoming one of the major importers of defence equipment, there is an urgent need to refine the process and make it more effective, without compromising on transparency. Though the DPP stipulates a timeframe for accomplishing every stage of this laborious procurement activity, once the AoN has been accorded, it does not elaborate on the sub-activities that make up each stage nor does it stipulate any timeframe for pre-RFP activities. Any introspection in the delays in defence procurement reveal that the

SQR forms the most important stage of the procurement and is a major bottleneck in the entire process. Thus, there is a need to define the sub-activities for each stage of procurement besides defining the activities prior to the RFP which are not addressed in the DPP. In addition, for effective monitoring of the procurement process, it is essential that the inter-related activities are closely monitored by an effective management tool that can provide real time assessment of the progress, identify the possible delays, provide an insight to the impact of delay in any stage, with its cascading impact on subsequent stages and, above all, provide the necessary feedback to keep the entire procurement actions on track.

Each capital procurement case has a definite beginning and an end that need to be accomplished within an envisaged timeframe and, hence, can be considered equivalent to a project. By definition, a project is any task which has a definite beginning and an end, requires resources for each separate but inter-dependent activity which must be accomplished to achieve the objectives. Thus, all procurement cases fulfil this definition in totality as they have a beginning and an end, a definite objective, can be broken down into identifiable activities, need team work, have to be completed by a target date, and, above all, involve uncertainties and risk.

India's annual defence acquisition budget is likely to exceed INR one lakh crore by 2016-17 while overall acquisition and support for the Indian armed forces is set to subsume more than US$ 150 billion in the coming decade, thus, its competent management is imperative. Acquisition trends of the past ten years paint a dismal picture. There is an urgent need to coopt contemporary international best practices into the acquisition process. There has already been a number of revisions of the DPP starting 1992 when it emerged as a rudimentary acquisition guideline. The need of the hour is implementation of the exhaustive recommendations arrived at through years of research involving all the stakeholders by various high level committees on acquisition reforms.

As discussed in the previous chapters, the modernisation and streamlining of the defence procurement and production systems are naturally related to the higher direction of defence decision-making, a realisation occurring consequent to the Kargil War. It was felt that decision-makers in both the government and the military forces will have to be more deliberate and methodical in their approach to capability building. This will lead to undertaking restructuring of higher defence management functions in a number of areas. Unfortunately, while implementing these, only half measures have been adopted. Ideally, capability acquisition should follow a top-down approach, but the present system continues to rely on the bottom-up approach. The acquisition process is not driven by macro aspects like national aims, national interests, national strategy, military strategy and force structure requirements flowing out of such a strategy. Instead, a mere operational directive issued by the Raksha Mantri forms the basis for the LTIPP.

The existing defence acquisition process is fraught with unacceptable and undue delays at all stages and a large percentage of the acquisition schemes result in foreclosure. Procedural propriety and integrity have overtaken the primary aim of effecting positive and timely procurement. Since the inception of a structured organisation and procurement in 2002, the number of acquisition schemes that have fructified has been limited. Even in these success stories, what can be credited to the procedure are mainly repeat procurements which involve fewer stages than a fresh acquisition. Year after year, success is measured in cash outgo which does not represent the true picture of modernisation attained by the armed forces. High value procurements are effected through inter-governmental deals which provide the saving grace to reduce the unexpended portion of budgetary allotments for modernisation. The procurement procedure has seen six amendments in a short period of nine years but even these have not provided any significant enhancement in the effectiveness. The Indian acquisition process, being in the nascent stage, needs to incorporate direction from the higher defence organisation, integrated planning, a professionally qualified and equipped structure, provision of a level playing field to the private industry, and overcoming its cumbersome procedures by giving it more flexibility which would help in informed decision-making.

As a ***first step***, an outcome-based framework needs to be put in place, along with a capability development executive on the lines suggested in this report. This will bring to the table flexibility, responsiveness and analysis-based decision-making. This will also enable management of risks and provide the ability to obviate delays and cost over-runs arising out of risk avoidance, and eventually lead to improving timeframes and outcomes of procurement. ***The second step*** would be strengthening the performance management framework among various overlapping functions of planning, budgeting, and acquisition, which will help establish the accountability of individuals and teams. The ***third step*** would be to streamline the procurement structure, making it an integrated, multi-disciplinary, specialised body on the lines of similar organisations existing globally for making procurement decisions. As the foundation for a system that facilitates timely delivery of military products and services at best value for money is laid, the focus will shift from compliance to risk management and achievement of the desired outcomes. While the organisational challenges are being addressed, a higher direction, that of integrating defence in the overall national development agenda, can be obtained to build a responsive defence procurement system geared towards achieving defined national strategic objectives.

The prevailing acquisition environment, encumbered by a bottom-up aggregation process, precludes effective control of expenditure through top-down strategic guidance. The size and budgetary demands of acquisition plans and the low availability of resources dictate prioritisation of projects which eventually leads to time and cost over-runs in their eventual fructification. A need for clarity of roles and accountability is, thus, of immense value in managing defence acquisition programmes. The policy dimension of defence acquisition is being addressed adequately with yet another version of the DPP on the horizon. The private sector too is upbeat with the recent pronouncements on the policy front which has spurred greater representation of both major and minor players into the defence manufacturing sector. This would, no doubt, go a long way in reducing India's import dependence for its defence requirements in the long term. What remains unaddressed is the structure that underpins this policy. The SHQ and the various wings of the MoD involved with acquisition need to operate in unison to realise the common objective of excogitating capabilities for the Indian armed forces in an acceptable cost and timeframe. This can only be achieved by inducting capability managers at the planning stage and heralding a project management vertical in the present acquisition structure. The project managers will have to possess state-of-the-art programme management operating and monitoring skills and the requisite authority to report to the organisational apex in the MoD. Such programme managers will need to be inducted from the corporate sector or academia where these roles are being routinely performed. In the absence of a programme management initiative, as described above, any prospect of reforming defence capital acquisition in India will remain a mirage.

Notes

1. "Review of Acquisition for the Secretary of State for Defence: An Independent Report by Bernard Gray", www.bipsolutions. com/docstore/ Review Acquisition Grayreport.pdf..
2. "First Principles Review, Creating One Defence", Australian Defence Forces, April 2015http:// www.defence. gov.au/Publications /Reviews/ First principles/Docs/FirstPrinciplesReviewB.pdf
3. "Committee of Experts for Amendment to DPP-2013 Including Formulation of Policy Framework", http://www.mod.nic.in/ writereaddata/ Reportddp. pdf. Accessed at 2100 hrs, on September 18, 2015.
4. The aspect of refinement of structures and accountability through programme management has been originally presented in a joint study carried out by the author along with C R Mohan and presented in the UCC in 2013.

5. CR Mohan, "Maintenance Evaluation Trials: Delight or Nightmare", *Defence Management Journal*, August 2012.
6. Incorporation of such modern management measures would require appropriate amendments to Schedule I F, Chapter 1, Annexure I to Schedule F, Para 16 of Appendix L to Schedule I, Article 5 of Chapter 5
7. Defence Material Organisation, Australian Government, http://www.defence.gov.au/dmo/

